Kiddiwalks

IN
DORSET

Nigel Vile

COUNTRYSIDE BOOKS
NEWBURY BERKSHIRE

First published 2008
Revised and updated 2014
© Nigel Vile, 2008

COUNTRYSIDE BOOKS
3 Catherine Road
Newbury, Berkshire

To view our complete range of books,
please visit us at
www.countrysidebooks.co.uk

ISBN 978 1 84674 067 1

Designed by Peter Davies, Nautilus Design
Produced by The Letterworks Ltd., Reading
Typeset by Jean Cussons Typesetting, Diss, Norfolk
Printed by Berforts Information Press, Oxford

All material for the manufacture of this
book was sourced from sustainable forests.

Contents

Contents

PUBLISHER'S NOTE

We hope that you obtain considerable enjoyment from this book; great care has been taken in its preparation. Although at the time of publication all routes followed public rights of way or permitted paths, diversion orders can be made and permissions withdrawn.

We cannot, of course, be held responsible for such diversion orders and any inaccuracies in the text which result from these or any other changes to the routes nor any damage which might result from walkers trespassing on private property. We are anxious though that all details covering the walks are kept up to date and would therefore welcome information from readers which would be relevant to future editions.

The simple sketch maps that accompany the walks in this book are based on notes made by the author whilst checking out the routes on the ground. They are designed to show you how to reach the start, to point out the main features of the overall circuit and they contain a progression of numbers that relate to the paragraphs of the text.

However, for the benefit of a proper map, we do recommend that you purchase the relevant Ordnance Survey sheet covering your walk. The Ordnance Survey maps are widely available, especially through booksellers and local newsagents.

Introduction

Being a writer of walking guidebooks, I am often asked for advice or recommendations for routes. This is particularly the case with friends with young families who, as childless couples, enjoyed a few hours in the great outdoors, a freedom that parenthood has curtailed. 'It must be a short walk, not too many hills and with something to interest the children along the way.' There is usually a footnote, too, that the walk must have a family-friendly pub or teashop, as much for mum or dad as the children!

The emphasis in this book of 'Kiddiwalks' matches the above specification almost perfectly. Do not expect Herculean treks of Wainwright proportions or you will be sadly disappointed. The objective is to provide relatively short and undemanding circular walks with a variety of attractions to stimulate the interest of youngsters. It may be the ever-popular stream or river, it could be a long barrow or hillfort, possibly a beach or safe rock scramble. With distances that range between 1 and 3 miles, there are routes here that will suit everyone from toddlers to top juniors, as well as their parents and grandparents.

Some of my first visits to Dorset were as a teacher, accompanying groups of children on geography fieldwork trips. Not being a geography specialist, I would stand bewildered as youngsters were told to measure the various dimensions of no fewer than 150 pebbles at various points along Chesil Beach! The logic behind the exercise was lost on me, as I cast my eyes across a landscape that invited exploration rather than hypothesis testing.

Later visits were in the form of family holidays – to Swanage, Eype, Kimmeridge and Lyme Regis – when ranging poles, clinometers and metre rules could be left safely behind in the storeroom. This gave the opportunity to explore the rich varieties of landscape that the county has to offer the visitor – the rugged cliffs of Purbeck, the sheer spectacle of Chesil Beach, the crumbling coastline of west Dorset, the lonely Dorset Downs, the unique heathlands and the splendours of Cranborne Chase. Add to this the manmade features – vast hillforts, picture postcard villages, hill figures, delightful country inns and elements of industrial archaeology – and you have a county that only the most world-weary would find dull.

AREA MAP SHOWING THE LOCATIONS OF THE WALKS

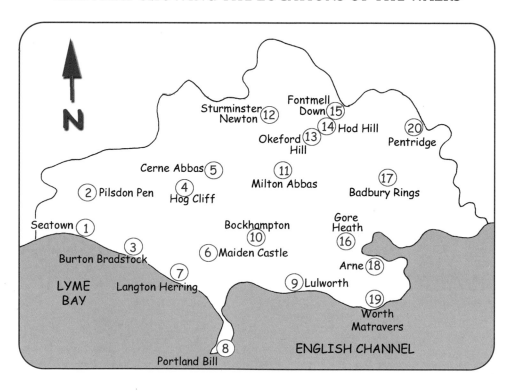

Introduction

Each walk is presented in as user-friendly a manner as possible. There is firstly an outline of the route, emphasising the features that youngsters will find most interesting. This is followed by a summary of the key information such as the distance and timing for the walk, how to get to the start point, parking and refreshment facilities. The nature of the terrain is also indicated, enabling you to decide if a particular walk is suitable for your youngster. The sketch maps that accompany the walk directions are designed to guide you around the route but I do recommend that you also take with you the relevant OS map, details of which are given. Background notes on the places and sights along the way are included, along with a special 'Fun Things to See and Do' section, detailing activities of particular interest for children to enhance their enjoyment of the walk.

My own children are now in their teens and early twenties, and have a penchant for rather more demanding routes. Crib Goch and Tryfan in Snowdonia, for example, excite and appeal far more to young adults than a 2-mile stroll along a riverbank! These routes, however, were some of their favourites in their formative years, and I am sure that it was these short circuits with their 'kiddy-friendly' attractions that instilled in them a love of the great outdoors. It is so important that children are not force-fed adult expeditions at a young age, or a negative attitude towards walking will be inevitable. With these thoughts in mind, I commend these routes to you and your families.

Nigel Vile

1

Seatown

Literal Highpoint

On the path above Seatown.

Seatown lies at the end of a narrow cul-de-sac lane, a mile or so south of Chideock. It is a perfect place to take the children who will enjoy the opportunity to paddle in the water and play on the shingle beach after this superb walk to the top of Golden Cap. At 626 ft above sea-level it is the highest cliff in southern England. From the top of Golden Cap, the views across the whole of Lyme Bay are exceptional so remember to carry some binoculars.

Getting there *Leave the A35 at Chideock, between Bridport and Lyme Regis, and follow the unclassified lane that runs south to the coast at Seatown. Park in the village car park alongside the beach (fee payable).*

Length of walk 2 miles
Time 2 hours
Terrain This is a relatively challenging walk, to the top of Golden Cap and back so most suitable for children aged five and over.

Start/Parking The public car park at Seatown just above the shingle beach alongside the Anchor Inn (GR 420918).
Maps OS Explorer 116 or OS Landranger 193.
Refreshments The Anchor Inn at Seatown, which has a splendid location, overlooking the shingle beach in the shadow of the Golden Cap.

❶ Leave the car park and turn right along the lane leading back towards Chideock. In 350 yards, turn left along a track signposted to Langdon Hill. Follow this

The Walk

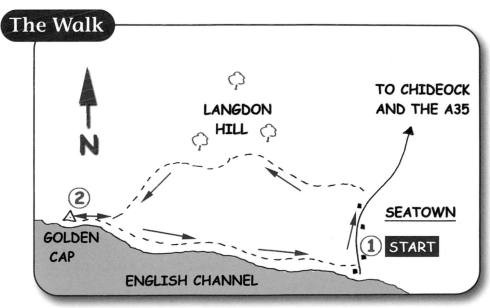

TO CHIDEOCK
AND THE A35

LANGDON
HILL

N

②
GOLDEN
CAP

SEATOWN

① START

ENGLISH CHANNEL

1

enclosed track uphill towards the woodland at the top of Langdon Hill, ignoring any right turns along the way. Just before the hilltop, the path passes through a gateway and continues around the southern edge of the woodland. Where the trees end, follow the path ahead signposted to Golden Cap. The route is clearly visible – it involves crossing two fields and stiles – before climbing to what is the highest point on the south coast of England.

2 The return to Seatown is along the Coast Path, which is both visible and well signposted. Should you need directions –

◆ Fun Things to See and Do ◆

Golden Cap will test the energies of young children – and their parents! Mark Wallington wrote of his ascent of the clifftop in his book *500 Mile Walkies*, a humorous account of walking the South West Coast Path with his dog Boogie. His strategy for the ascent was quite simple: 'Golden Cap could be conquered with the right tactics. Walk a few yards, stop, have a drink, a hunk of chocolate and a little lie down, then walk another few yards. An hour and a whole bar of Galaxy later, I finally scrambled up to the summit.'

Back on **the beach** in Seatown, see how many small pieces of coloured glass – made smooth by the sea – the children can find amongst the pebbles and shingle. Fill a small container with these colourful pieces of glass and they will have an attractive memento of their visit. There are also many flat **pebbles** along the beach, superb for skimming, as well as all manner of **shells** to identify and collect. You may also be lucky enough to see anglers landing bass and mackerel, with Seatown beach being an excellent spot for fishing. Behind the beach lie crumbling sandstone cliffs, evidence of the erosive power of the sea.

retrace your steps back downhill to the first stile. Rather than continuing back to Langdon Hill, bear right to another stile, before crossing three further fields to reach a belt of trees. Follow the path through this tree cover, then cross one final field to join the lane in Seatown where a right turn returns you to the car park.

The Anchor Inn, Seatown.

◆ Background Notes ◆

The **Golden Cap** is the centrepiece of a 2,000 acre estate owned and managed by the National Trust. The property consists of hill, farmland, cliff, undercliff and beach between Charmouth and Eypemouth. From the flat summit of Golden Cap, whose name comes from the coloration of the cliff's summit, where golden sandstone and clumps of gorse bushes reflect a golden hue in bright sunlight, the views across Lyme Bay are quite marvellous. Be sure to walk beyond the trig point to the western end of the summit, where a superb seascape will await you.

It comes as no surprise to discover that this lonely section of the coast was populated by smugglers in centuries past, with **Seatown** being a centre of their activities. Many a keg of brandy would have been landed at Seatown under cover of darkness, with the local network of tracks and lanes being used to distribute the contraband to nearby villages.

Today the village is an altogether more peaceful place. Thatched cottages, fashioned from honey-coloured stone, line the main street, which ends on the coast alongside the 18th-century Anchor Inn. Shore-fishing is an especially popular pastime here.

Pilsdon Pen

Summit Else

The trig point on Pilsdon Pen.

West Dorset – remote and accessible by generally narrow and winding lanes – has never been as popular with walkers as the better-known east of the county. This makes for a rather unspoiled landscape that is truly far from the madding crowd. This walk explores the open hills of Pilsdon, with expansive outlooks at every turn and youngsters will feel a real sense of achievement when they stand on the top of this ancient hillfort.

Getting there *Turn off the A3066 at Beaminster and follow the B3163 to Broadwindsor. In the village, turn left onto the B3164, signposted to Lyme Regis. In 2 miles, park in a lay-by on the left at the foot of Pilsdon Pen, which is on the right-hand side of the road.*

Length of walk 2½ miles
Time Up to 2 hours
Terrain Although this walk explores one of Dorset's high points, the start of the walk is already over 700 ft above sea-level. The ascent of Pilsdon Pen is therefore gentle and gradual, and well within the capabilities of most youngsters.
Start/Parking The lay-by below Pilsdon Pen (GR 414009).
Maps OS Explorer 116 or OS Landranger 193.
Refreshments The green open spaces of Pilsdon Pen are ideal for a picnic. Alternatively, head back into Broadwindsor and seek out the White Lion pub, which offers good home-cooked food and a children's menu.

The Walk

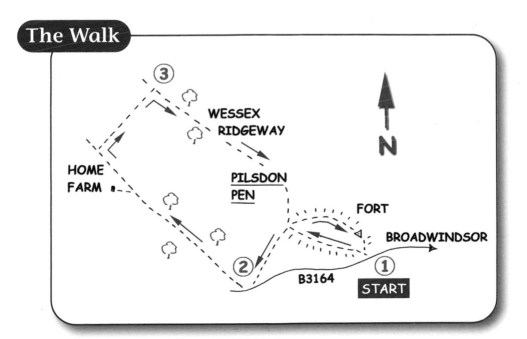

1 Cross the road and a stile opposite, and follow a footpath up towards Pilsdon Pen. In 75 yards, just past some steps and wooden fencing, the path reaches a junction. Turn left, and walk along the south-western flank of the hillside, with the hilltop up on

◆ Fun Things to See and Do ◆

Round barrows are probably the most widespread and numerous class of archaeological monument in Europe. At its most basic, a round barrow is simply a roughly hemispherical mound of soil, stone, and redeposited bedrock heaped over a central burial. It is interesting to look around the hillfort enclosure on top of Pilsdon Pen and see how many of these old burial mounds there are. Archaeologists often excavate areas such as this and, as well as skeletal remains, find pottery and arrowheads and other personal effects.

The information board at the entrance to Pilsdon Pen tells of the **rich and varied wildlife** to be found on this hilltop. The mammals depicted include a weasel, fox and badger, whilst the reptiles include a grass snake and a lizard. There are birds of prey, as well as orchids and a variety of butterflies. The information board also describes in detail how the ramparts on this high hilltop are part of an **ancient fort**, which was located on this site because of the fine outlook it provided across the surrounding countryside. By the time that weary invaders had reached the lower slopes of Pilsdon Pen, the residents of the hilltop would be ready to attack with a volley of rocks and stones and arrows!

Having climbed to the summit of Pilsdon Pen, you are at the **second highest point in Dorset**. Before you get too excited, however, perhaps things should be put into perspective. Pilsdon Pen is 909 ft above sea-level, Snowdon – the highest peak in England and Wales – comes in at 3,560 ft, some four times higher!

The amazing view from the top of Pilsdon Pen.

the right. Keep on this path – it shortly borders a line of beech trees on the left – for 350 yards to a gate in the far corner of the Pilsdon Pen National Trust enclosure. Beyond this gate, turn left and follow a track for 300 yards down to a lane. Turn right and, almost immediately, pass through a gateway on the right to join a bridleway.

2 Follow this right-of-way across the left edges of three fields before reaching a track. Continue for 200 yards to a junction where another track goes off on the left. Ignore this left turn, keeping ahead for a further 50 yards to a fork. Bear right, and follow the higher level track ahead for 250 yards to a point where there is a gateway ahead and a gate on the right. Pass through the gateway on the right, and walk up the left-hand edge of the field ahead to a gateway in its top left corner.

3 Beyond this gate, turn right and follow the right edge of a hilltop field to a handgate in its corner. Cross the middle of the next field on a permissive path to a handgate opposite, before

continuing along the right edge of the next field to another handgate. Bear half-right across the middle of the next field, making for a gate in the right-hand field boundary almost in the far corner of the field. Beyond this gate, follow a path that drops downhill back to the entrance gate into the National Trust enclosure passed at the outset. Go through this gateway, and follow the path that veers left uphill to reach the hilltop enclosure. Turn right, and walk along to the trig point on Pilsdon Pen. To the left of the trig point, follow a path that drops downhill back to a stile and the lay-by.

NB: For a short walk, on reaching the end of the line of beech trees in point 1, turn right and climb to the top of Pilsdon Pen, returning the same way.

◆ Background Notes ◆

Pilsdon Pen provides a foretaste of the tors of Devon, treeless and formed on decaying granite. For many years, it was thought to be the literal high point in the county, standing at 909 ft above sea-level. Neighbouring **Lewesdon Hill** was believed to be some 15 ft lower, although recent measurements have shown this green and curvaceous hilltop to reach 915 ft! Both hills stand guard on the northern slopes of the lush Marshwood Vale, and look in a southerly direction towards Lyme Bay.

As recently as the late 1970s, guidebooks were still relating that Pilsdon Pen was the highest point in Dorset. Ralph Whiteman – in his volume *Portrait of Dorset* – described nearby Lewesdon Hill as a 'noble place, crowned with trees and only slightly lower than the bare top of its neighbour Pilsdon Pen'. There is an old saying that goes 'as much akin as Lewesdon and Pilsdon', the implication being that these two Dorset hills are very similar. The truth is quite different; Lewesdon is wooded, rounded and roughly conical, and Pilsdon is bare and rises like a cliff from the surrounding vale. As Whiteman puts it: 'They are not alike in any particular except in being two pleasant hills which are landmarks for half the county.'

Pilsdon Pen is also the site of a rather fine hillfort. The local archaeological guidebooks point out an Iron Age fort with two ramparts, an internal area of nearly 8 acres and original entrances at the south-east, the south-west and possibly at the north. There is a series of five round barrows at the southern end of the site, whilst near the middle of the fort four banks form a square enclosure. Recent excavation – according to Pevsner writing in 1972 – has shown that the banks cover a series of narrow rectangular buildings that enclose and lie over a series of hut circles. Pilsdon Pen is one of several hillforts in the area built by the Celtic tribe of the Durotriges to settle border disputes with the Dumnonii to the west.

3

Burton Bradstock

Jurassic Coast

Burton Bradstock beach is an ideal playground for children.

The Dorset and East Devon Coast World Heritage Site is England's first natural World Heritage Site. Known as the Jurassic Coast, it covers 95 miles of truly stunning coastline from east Devon to Dorset, with rocks recording 185 million years of the Earth's history. World Heritage status was achieved because of the site's unique insight into the Earth Sciences as it clearly depicts a geological 'walk through time' spanning the Triassic, Jurassic and Cretaceous periods.

This short walk provides the perfect introduction to this dramatic stretch of coastline, exploring a section to the south of the village of Burton Bradstock. Down on Burton Beach at low tide, the fine shingle gives way to sand, so be sure to pack a bucket and spade in the boot of the car.

Kiddiwalks in Dorset

3

Getting there *Burton Bradstock lies on the B3157 between Bridport and Weymouth. On the eastern edge of the village, turn into Beach Road and drive down to the National Trust car park by the beach at Burton Bradstock, free to National Trust members.*

Length of walk 2 miles
Time 1½ hours
Terrain A coastal walk with one ascent onto – and descent from – Burton Cliff. It is best suited to slightly older children since the clifftop part of the walk is unfenced in places with a 120-ft drop down to the beach below. Do keep any young children under close supervision at all times on this section.
Start/Parking The car park behind Burton Beach (GR 493888).
Maps OS Outdoor Leisure 15 or OS Landranger 194.
Refreshments The justifiably popular Hive Beach Café at Burton Bradstock which is open all year round offers salmon fishcakes, perfectly grilled fish and salad or simple tea and buns served either inside or at tables perched on the grassy slopes above the beach.

The Walk

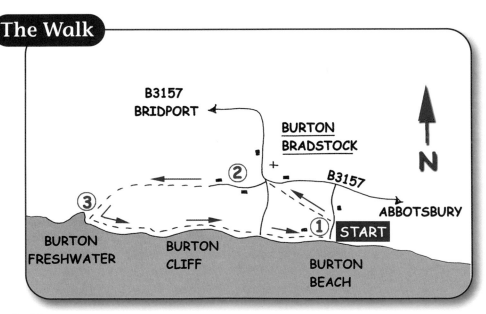

1 As you approach the National Trust car park from the B3157, you pass a large grassy area on the right – it is often used as an overflow car park. Cross this grassy area to a handgate in the opposite hedgerow, about 50 yards to the right of the Burton Cliff Hotel. Beyond this handgate – which is hidden behind the hedge – walk across to another handgate in the far right corner of the field ahead. In the following field, bear half-right to a stile in the far right corner of the field. Cross this stile, and drop downhill to a back lane. Turn right and, almost immediately, left into Southover.

2 Walk to the end of this cul-de-sac lane, before continuing along an enclosed path to a stile and open field. Go ahead along the bottom right edge of this field for 300 yards to a junction, then continue along the path waymarked to Burton Beach. Follow this path to a stile just before the sea and Burton Freshwater.

◆ Fun Things to See and Do ◆

Put **youngsters, water, the sea and rocks** together and there is no limit to the fun that can be enjoyed. At Burton Freshwater, there are some fine boulders that are perfectly designed for a good rock scramble. The walk across Burton Cliff will have inquisitive youngsters nudging towards the cliff edge to see just how far down the drop is. A word of warning – some of the clifftop path is unfenced and getting too close to the edge is extremely dangerous. Better to walk a short distance away from the cliff edge, and discover the coastal flora that lies along the way. See if anyone can spot thrift or rock samphire, alexanders or red valerian. Back on Burton Beach, there is shallow water to paddle in, shells aplenty to collect and the delightful Hive Beach Café. All the ingredients for a perfect day out by the seaside.

3

Burton Freshwater.

3 Cross the stile, turn left and follow the Coast Path across Burton Cliff back towards Burton Beach. In ¾ mile, keep on the path as it drops down past the Burton Cliff Hotel to reach the beach. Turn left back to the car park.

◆ Background Notes ◆

The first part of the walk – from Burton Beach across country to Burton Freshwater - is a fairly undistinguished stroll that connects up the two ends of the dramatic coastal section of the route. It does bring a rather good view across the village of Burton Bradstock – set against a backdrop of North Hill and Bredy North Hill – but in all honesty is merely a prelude to an encounter with the Jurassic Coast. The place name **Burton Bradstock**, incidentally, does have an interesting origin. In Saxon times, the village was called Brideton or Bridetone meaning the village of the River Bride, which evolved to Bridetona as recorded in the Domesday Book of 1086. Bradstock came from Bradenstoke, named after Bradenstoke Priory in Wiltshire to which the village once belonged. The present name appears to be a corruption of the two.

The first part of the coast that the walk encounters is **Burton Freshwater**. This is where the River Bride enters the sea, with its meandering course producing amazing patterns in the shingle that lines the foreshore. From Burton Freshwater, the coastal path climbs onto **Burton Cliff**. The views across Lyme Bay are quite dramatic, as is the view towards the Isle of Portland in the east. It is not until the path drops down onto the beach at Burton, however, that the true nature of Burton Cliff can be fully appreciated. These vertical sandstone cliffs, with remarkable striations, present an amazing picture especially when illuminated by the golden rays of a sunset. **Burton Beach** itself lies at the extreme western end of Chesil Beach, the remarkable coastal feature that extends for some 18 miles to the Isle of Portland (see also Walk 7). The process of longshore drift means that only the finest of pebbles end up on Burton Beach, with the pebble size steadily increasing as Chesil Beach approaches Portland. It is said that local sailors and fishermen who were washed up at night on Chesil Beach could pinpoint their exact location by the size of the local pebbles!

4

Hog Cliff

In Reserve

Inquisitive locals at Hog Cliff.

The hardest thing about this walk is actually finding the start! Hog Cliff Farm, alongside which there is a parking area, is located behind a belt of trees on the crest of a hill on the A37 between Dorchester and Yeovil. Dorset is renowned for its chalk downland, with the Hog Cliff reserve being an archetypal example of such a habitat. Whether it is a rich array of flora or a splash of colour associated with a wide variety of butterfly species, Hog Cliff National Nature Reserve will not disappoint … once you have pinpointed its location!

Getting there *Follow the A37 north from Dorchester for 6 miles to a garage called Long Ash Service Station. Continue for another ½ mile to the entrance to Hyde Crook Nursing Home, before climbing uphill for another ½ mile to pass lay-bys on either side of the road. In 100 yards, an easily missed track leaves the A37 on the left – there is a bridleway sign. Turn left and park by this track, which lies alongside Hog Cliff Farm, which is hidden from the main road by tree cover.*

Length of walk 2½ miles
Time Up to 2 hours

Terrain An easy walk until the short hill section described in point 3. The climb could be avoided by simply retracing your steps back up the main track to the parking area. This would make the walk suitable for children of all ages.
Start/Parking The rough parking area alongside Hog Cliff Farm (GR 620976).
Maps OS Explorer 117 or OS Landranger 194.
Refreshments I would recommend taking a picnic to Hog Cliff to enjoy somewhere along the way. Alternatively, drive north along the A37 for 1½ miles before taking a left turn to Maiden Newton and the Chalk and Cheese Inn.

◆ Background Notes ◆

Hog Cliff National Nature Reserve is a chalk downland area comprising three separate sites centred on Hog Cliff Hill. The reserve has downland slopes with rich grassland communities typical of the chalk of west-central Dorset. Areas of scrub and small areas of woodland add diversity to the site. The grassland supports a wide range of grasses, herbs and flowering plants such as sheep's fescue, meadow oat, rockrose, small scabious, devil's-bit scabious, chalk milkwort and betony, whilst over 100 species of fungus have been recorded on the site. Butterflies bring a lively splash of colour to the reserve during the summer. These include the rare adonis blue and marsh fritillary, and more common species such as the green hair-streak, common blue, gatekeeper, grizzled skipper and dingy skipper.

The Walk

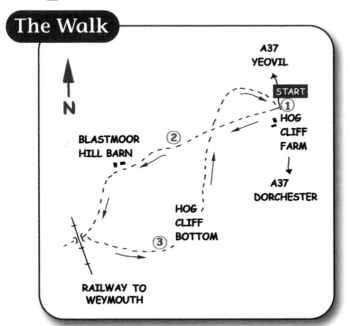

the left edge of the next field towards Blastmoor Hill Barn. On the far side of the field, beyond a gate, follow a grassy path alongside some paddocks to a gate by some barns on the right. Beyond these buildings, continue downhill on a track to reach the Bristol to Weymouth railway line in 250 yards. Just before the railway, turn left into a field and, in a few yards, bear left through a newly planted area of tree cover. Continue following what is a bridleway through Hog Cliff Bottom to a handgate in the far-left corner of the field, and another Hog Cliff information board.

❶ Walk along the broad chalk track running downhill from the A37. At the bottom of the hill, pass through a gateway – a Hog Cliff information board is in the field on the right – and continue along the track through the valley bottom. Ignoring a stile on the right, keep on the track as it climbs uphill to a gate. Beyond this gate, keep on the track as it crosses the hilltop before entering an arable field.

❷ Follow the left edge of this field around to a gate in the opposite boundary, almost in the corner. Beyond this gate, follow

❸ Beyond the handgate, follow the left edge of two fields in the heart of the Hog Cliff reserve to a gate and the track walked along at the outset. Pass through a stile in the fence opposite – slightly to the right – and walk ahead for 20 yards before turning right to follow a grassy path uphill. At the top of the climb, walk ahead to a fence, turn right and continue along to a stile. Follow the left edge of the next field, walking around any bushes that obstruct your passage across what is access land, to a stile in the far corner of the field. Climb the steps beyond this stile to return to the parking area.

The entrance to the Nature Reserve.

◆ Fun Things to See and Do ◆

National Nature Reserves (NNRs) are places where wildlife comes first. They were established to protect the most important areas for wildlife in Britain. This does not mean they are 'no-go areas' for people – just that we must be careful not to damage the wildlife of these fragile places. Every NNR is nationally important in that they are all among the best examples of a particular habitat. In the case of Hog Cliff, the **flowers and butterflies** are what attract visitors from far and wide. A fun activity could be to see how many letters of the alphabet can be matched against a species at Hog Cliff. 'S' could be for scabious, for example, whilst 'C' could be for the common blue butterfly. To help with this, be sure to take a good spotter's guide with you.

If your youngsters like **watching trains go up and down**, the railway line from Bristol to Weymouth runs along the south-western end of the Hog Cliff reserve. This is one of the few rural lines that escaped the Beeching cutbacks of the 1960s but the trains are few and far between, with eight services in each direction on a typical weekday. Consult a railway timetable before your visit, and time your walk accordingly, and you will be able to enjoy the sight of railway traffic on one of England's most picturesque routes.

5

Cerne Abbas

The Giant

A leafy glade along the way.

Cerne Abbas, nestling deep in the Cerne Valley, is a beautiful stone, brick and flint village that must surely rank as one of the most handsome settlements in all of Dorset. To the north of Cerne Abbas rises Giant Hill, on whose slopes is carved a massive 180 ft long hill figure … who is not noted for his modesty, something which youngsters find particularly amusing! Beyond the Giant lies an ancient earthwork – known as the 'Trendle' – that was the site of ancient May Day rituals until recent times. An intriguing walk across the mysterious Wessex landscape.

Getting there *Cerne Abbas lies 8 miles north of Dorchester, just off the A352. Drive into the centre of the village from the main road and park on the main street somewhere between the New Inn and the Royal Oak.*

Length of walk 2½ miles
Time 2 hours
Terrain Steep climbs onto – and down from – Giant Hill,

combined with some level hilltop walking. Younger children may clamour for the occasional piggy back.

Start/Parking The main street in Cerne Abbas (GR 665011).
Maps OS Explorer 117 or OS Landranger 194.
Refreshments There are pubs and tea rooms in Cerne Abbas. Giant Hill, with its many vantage points, would be an excellent spot for a picnic.

The Walk

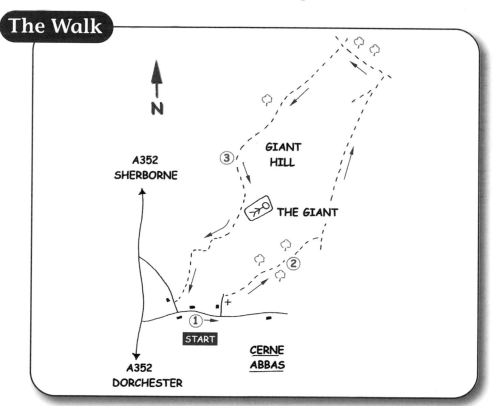

5

1 Walk along the main street in Cerne Abbas to the Royal Oak pub and turn left into Abbey Street. At the top of Abbey Street, pass through a gate on the right into a churchyard. Follow the path to the left across to an archway and a gate, leave the churchyard and walk over an open grassy space to a stile opposite at the entrance to some woodland. At a junction just past

◆ Fun Things to See and Do ◆

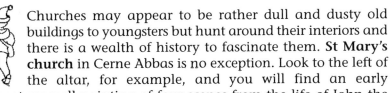

Churches may appear to be rather dull and dusty old buildings to youngsters but hunt around their interiors and there is a wealth of history to fascinate them. **St Mary's church** in Cerne Abbas is no exception. Look to the left of the altar, for example, and you will find an early 14th-century wall painting of four scenes from the life of John the Baptist, whilst the east window contains 16 stained-glass shields from the Brownyng family. The church tower is embellished with a number of rather fine examples of gargoyles, whilst to the left of the porch door is an open mouthed gargoyle which is the chimney outlet for a fireplace in the priest's chamber. One other artefact to look out for is a stone coffin and lid that came from the abbey that once existed in the village. If ecclesiastical architecture is lost on your youngsters, then leave them in the stocks that lie in the street outside the church!

Some **wonderful wild flowers** can be found on chalk hills, including orchids and cowslips, harebells and trefoil, and Giant Hill is no exception. The floral displays here in spring and summer are quite exceptional.

Bubbling out from these chalk hills are a series of springs that eventually form the local river – known unsurprisingly as the Cerne. The **Cerne's shallow waters** are followed towards journey's end, so it is well worth bringing along a towel on warm days so that youngsters can enjoy a refreshing paddle.

this stile, turn right and follow a path around the edge of the woodland for 250 yards.

Heading for the hilltop.

2 Keep on this path as it bears right to drop down to a junction. Turn left, and follow what is a bridleway for ½ mile, climbing to the open ground high on Giant Hill. On reaching a gate – a track comes in on the left at this point – keep ahead along the left edge of a hilltop field to a cattle compound. Immediately beyond this compound, turn left through a gate to follow a path waymarked to the Wessex Ridgeway. Cross the middle of a hilltop field to a crossroads of paths in 250 yards, and turn left along the path waymarked to the Cerne Giant. Follow this path across the middle of a hilltop field to a stile on the right in 300 yards.

3 Beyond this stile, follow the path to the left towards an area of scrubland. Keep on the path as it drops downhill through the scrubland to emerge onto the open hillside. Continue on the path as it descends to pass the bottom of the enclosure containing the Cerne Giant in 350 yards. Go down some steps to a junction, and turn right through a handgate along the path to Kettle Bridge. On reaching a junction by a barn, turn left; keep right at the next junction and continue to Kettle Bridge. Turn left just past the bridge and follow the River Cerne back into Cerne Abbas, the path reaching Mill Lane in 200 yards. Continue along Mill Lane to its junction with Duck Street. Turn left back to the main street in Cerne Abbas.

◆ Background Notes ◆

The hills above Cerne Abbas are formed of chalk, a type of limestone derived from the mineral calcite. It is produced under relatively deep marine conditions from the gradual accumulation of minute calcite plates (coccoliths) shed from micro-organisms called coccolithophores ... I'll leave you to explain that one to the youngsters! All over southern Britain, where there was chalk bedrock, local people in years gone by would remove the grass and topsoil to create shapes – usually horses but sometimes human figures as in the case of the **Cerne Abbas Giant**.

This depiction of a naked male is thought to be the work of the Romano-British. It was allegedly based upon the Roman mythical hero Hercules, who is always depicted carrying a club. The true nature of the figure can only be gauged from a viewpoint some way away from the actual walk route. The footpath running alongside the figure enables the visitor to obtain only a partial view of one of the country's best-known landmarks.

The village of **Cerne Abbas** has a long and illustrious history. A Benedictine abbey was founded here in the 10th century, the remains of which can be seen in the fields behind the church. St Mary's church itself is well worth a visit to see its 15th-century rood screen and the Jacobean pulpit with its canopy or 'tester'.

In the 18th century, a large brewing industry was established in the village to supply fine ales to hostelries in London. This explains the presence of several exceptional inns in what is a relatively small village.

Maiden Castle

On Guard

The remains of a Roman temple at Maiden Castle.

T homas Hardy was certainly impressed with this vast hillfort just a mile or so outside Dorchester. His description of what is widely held to be one of Europe's most impressive ancient monuments was eloquent indeed: 'It may be likened to an enormous, many limbed organism of an antediluvian time, lying lifeless, and covered with a thin green cloth, which hides its substance, while revealing its contour.' This is a hilltop walk across a deserted landscape that once positively hummed with the sound of human activity. Be sure to pick a fine, clear day, the hillfort site being particularly open and exposed.

Kiddiwalks in Dorset

6

Getting there *Follow the A35 around Dorchester to a roundabout where the A354 Weymouth road heads south. At this point, head north along the B3147 into the town centre. In ½ mile, turn left along an unclassified road waymarked to Maiden Castle. Follow this lane for 1¼ miles to the castle's car park.*

Length of walk 1½ miles
Time 1½ hours
Terrain The steep ramparts mean that this walk is better suited to older children. Toddlers would need to be kept on a very tight rein or face rolling down the castle's ramparts into deep ditches!

Start/Parking The Maiden Castle car park which is free (GR 669889).

Maps OS Outdoor Leisure 15 or OS Landranger 194.

Refreshments Why not take a picnic to enjoy on this majestic hilltop site? In high summer, there can be few better places to eat alfresco. Alternatively, if you return to the A35 and follow it in a westerly direction to its junction with the A37, you will find a McDonald's restaurant that will certainly please the youngsters.

The Walk

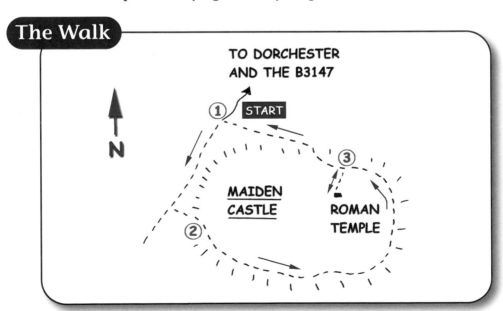

1 Leave the car park and follow the main well-worn path uphill towards the western edge of Maiden Castle. In 100 yards, pass through a gateway and continue to a second gate just before the ramparts. Continue ahead for 40 yards to the western entrance to the hillfort. Turn left by an information board, and follow a path uphill to a gateway immediately in front of the upper set of ramparts.

◆ Fun Things to See and Do ◆

With ramparts that extend to well over a mile in length – some rising to a height of over 20 feet – **Maiden Castle** is the perfect place for youngsters to re-enact the Roman Second Legion storming the fortress. Back in AD 45, there were many casualties during the actual battle, with bodies and possessions being scattered widely across the site. Be sure to pick a relatively safe part of the rampart to avoid a significant tumble and bruises! Many of the artefacts that date from this period can be seen in the Dorset County Museum in High West Street, Dorchester, including skeletal remains.

Given its high location, Maiden Castle is the perfect spot for **paragliding**. Youngsters – and their guardians – will enjoy watching the free-flying, foot launched aircraft. Pilots sit in a harness suspended below a fabric wing, whose shape is formed by the pressure of air entering vents in the front of the wing. Paragliding records make exceptional reading. The Slovenian-born Valic brothers set a world distance record of 426 km in South Africa in 2006, whilst the official record for height gain is held by Robbie Whittall of England. He gained 4,526 metres of height on a flight in South Africa in 1993. Neither record is likely to be beaten in the vicinity of Maiden Castle!

2 Beyond these gates, turn right and climb up onto the upper rampart. Follow this in an anti-clockwise direction around the hilltop. In ½ mile, just past the north-eastern corner of the hilltop, detour to the left to explore the remains of a Roman temple.

The path around the hillfort.

3 Return to the rampart, and continue for 100 yards to a stile and steep stepped path that drops down through the middle rampart and on down to the lower rampart. Below this lower rampart, follow a path to the left for 250 yards to a gate and a grassy enclosure. Cross this enclosure to return to the car park.

◆ Background Notes ◆

Maiden Castle sits proudly on top of a vast chalk hilltop to the south-west of Dorchester. From its lofty vantage point, it is easy to see why generations of settlers have targeted this strategic site as the prime location in the area. As early as 3,500 BC, a Neolithic camp occupied the hilltop. By 350 BC, Iron Age settlers had made Maiden Castle their home. The hilltop would have been covered with timber huts, surrounded by vast defences broken only by well-guarded gateways. Archaeologists estimate that as many as 500 people occupied the site, tilling the surrounding fields and tending their sheep and cattle.

In AD 45, **Vespasian's Second Legion** stormed the fortress and the hilltop fell into the hands of the Romans. The fighting was fierce, with the Romans facing an onslaught of sling stones – round pebbles gathered from Chesil Beach. The Second Legion won the day, however, and countless bodies were buried in the graveyard near the eastern entrance to the fort. On the site, the foundations of a Roman temple remain to this day.

Langton Herring and the Fleet

A Fine Lagoon

On the coast path.

The 18-mile long Chesil Beach extends from Portland westwards to Burton Bradstock. Between the beach and the Dorset mainland lies the Fleet, widely believed to be the best example of a lagoon in the British Isles. Its salt water is home to a rich array of seabirds, including a wide variety of waders. The whole area has rich literary associations, too, ranging from John Meade Falkner's *Moonfleet* – a tale of smuggling – to Ian McEwan's *On Chesil Beach* – a story of lost romance. From the attractive village of Langton Herring, this walk explores a fascinating section of the Fleet lagoon, with views towards the pebble ridge of Chesil Beach. This is truly a 5-star excursion.

Getting there *Leave the B3157 road to Abbotsbury and Bridport 8 miles west of Weymouth, and follow the unclassified road that heads west into Langton Herring. In ¾ mile, turn left by a telephone box and drive down to the Elm Tree Inn, where a sign says that walkers are allowed to park in the paddock alongside the pub.*

Length of walk 2½ miles
Time Up to 2 hours
Terrain An easy walk, with one short ascent from the coast back

into Langton Herring, suitable for all ages.
Start/Parking The Elm Tree Inn at Langton Herring (GR 614825).
Maps OS Outdoor Leisure 15 or Landranger 194.
Refreshments With the Elm Tree Inn allowing walkers free use of a paddock for parking, the publican should be rewarded with your custom. Weather permitting, the inn's excellent garden is a perfect place to rest awhile and linger following a walk along a unique stretch of the Dorset coastline.

The Walk

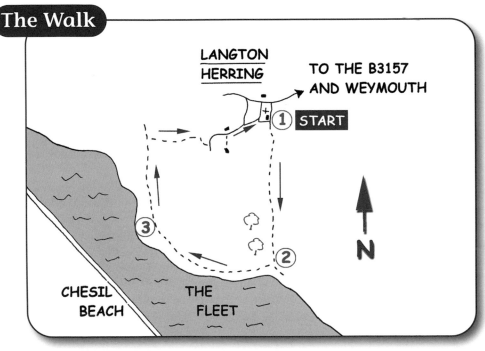

LANGTON
HERRING

TO THE B3157
AND WEYMOUTH

① START

③

②

N

CHESIL
BEACH

THE
FLEET

Langton Herring and the Fleet

1 Join the road outside the pub, turn right and walk the short distance to a junction. Keep ahead along a cul-de-sac lane for 100 yards to Fleet Way Cottage, just past a Methodist chapel on the left, turn left along the track waymarked to the Coast Path and Fleet, and continue for ½ mile down to the Fleet.

2 Turn right, and follow the Coast Path in the direction of Abbotsbury. In ½ mile, ignore a track on the right waymarked to Langton Herring, keeping ahead instead along the Coast Path. In 600 yards, the path reaches a fence. Turn right for 20 yards, before passing through a gateway on the left, still keeping on the Coast Path to Abbotsbury.

◆ Fun Things to See and Do ◆

Much of the fun on this walk involves water – so make sure that you have a towel in the trusty old rucksack. Along the edge of the Fleet, **the water is shallow and safe for a paddle**. It may look muddy in places, but it is totally harmless. The Fleet's shoreline is also littered with **shells**, including many belonging to oysters. This stretch of water has always had oyster beds, and they have even been immortalised in a poem:

> Oysters lying in the deep.
> Bedded down beneath the Fleet.
> Above salty waters swirl.
> A special one may hold a pearl.

The Fleet also attracts a wide variety of **seabirds**, with over 300 different species of bird having been recorded in the locality. On the lagoon itself, hundreds of diving ducks including pochards and tufted ducks plus smaller numbers of scaup, goldeneye and long-tailed ducks are usually present. Herons breed by the edge of the Fleet and other birds regularly seen include Canada geese, cormorants, coots, moorhens, and several species of grebe, kingfisher and snipe. Be sure to take a pair of binoculars and a good spotting guidebook on this walk.

3 Follow the left edges of the next three fields to a junction of paths. Turn right, and follow the path signposted to Langton Herring, climbing uphill alongside a boundary wall on the left. In the corner of the field, bear right along the end field boundary – the path soon bears left – to reach a stile. Cross this stile, and follow a track around to the left, still waymarked to Langton Herring. In 200 yards, keep left at a junction and

A tranquil scene on the Fleet.

continue for 40 yards to the next junction. Turn right and follow a road between stone properties to the next junction. Turn right past the village church, before keeping left at the next junction back to the Elm Tree Inn.

◆ Background Notes ◆

Chesil Beach has been described as 'the eighth wonder of the world' (see also Walk 3). The pebbles along the beach are finely graded, from the sands of Abbotsbury through to the boulders of Portland. It is even said that fishermen and smugglers in the past could tell whereabouts they had washed up on Chesil under cover of darkness by the size of the pebbles. The vast Fleet lagoon, which is enclosed by the beach between Portland and Abbotsbury, is popular with local fishermen on account of its fine mullet and bass, whilst bird-watchers will find plenty of interest in and around its waters.

One common species of bird on the Fleet is the **mute swan**. The swannery at nearby Abbotsbury contains the largest colony of managed swans in the world, and many of these birds find their way along to the section of the Fleet passed on this walk. What attracts so many mute swans to the Fleet is the presence of *Zostera marina*, their favourite variety of seaweed. The adult male is the largest British bird, weighing upwards of 20 pounds and measuring over 5 feet from the beak to the tail. To describe the swan as 'mute' is something of a misnomer. The adult birds all too readily snort, hiss or call, whilst the young cygnets are noted for their shrill piping.

8

Portland

Old Bill

Striding out on the walk.

The Isle of Portland is, in fact, a peninsula, linked to the mainland by a long strip of shingle known as Chesil Beach. Portland Bill is the southern tip of this peninsula, and is the site of rugged limestone cliffs, a pair of lighthouses and a number of small caves. 'The Bill' is also a magnet for a large number of seabirds. This is a wild and exhilarating excursion, with magnificent sea views, exciting rocky outcrops and interest at every turn.

Kiddiwalks in Dorset

 Getting there *Follow the A354 south from Weymouth – the road is signposted to Portland. Where this road ends at Easton, continue along the unclassified road signposted to Portland Bill. Park in the large public car park (fee payable) just before the prominent red and white lighthouse.*

Length of walk 2½ miles

Time 2 hours

Terrain A relatively flat and easy walk. With cliffs along the way, be sure to keep a close eye on the youngsters in your party.

Start/Parking The public car park at Portland Bill (GR 675683).

Maps OS Outdoor Leisure 15 or OS Landranger 194.

Refreshments There is an excellent seaside café at Portland Bill, as well as the Pulpit Inn, a family-friendly hostelry, where the emphasis is on fresh seafood.

The Walk

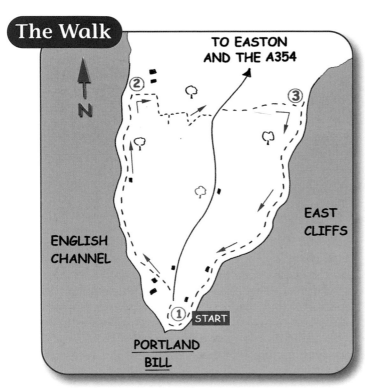

TO EASTON AND THE A354

N

ENGLISH CHANNEL

EAST CLIFFS

START

PORTLAND BILL

❶ Leave the car park at the northern end – the furthest end from the lighthouse – cross an MOD access road and walk over to the far end of the fence surrounding the MOD complex. Bear left across to the path that runs along the clifftops, and continue in a northerly direction for ½ mile to a marker stone, passing an old lighthouse along the way.

2 Turn right – the path is signposted to East Cliff – and follow a path around two sides of an open field to reach a junction, with a path going off on the right. Ignoring the right turn, continue for 100 yards to the next junction. Bear right, keep left at an early fork and follow a grassy path down to the Southwell to Portland Bill road. Turn left and, in 100 yards, right down a gated track waymarked to Longstone and Ope Quarry. Walk down to a crane on the Coast Path and turn right.

◆ Fun Things to See and Do ◆

The area around Portland Bill is the perfect place to introduce youngsters to a spot of **birdwatching**. Being surrounded by the English Channel, there are all manner of seabirds to look out for. These include a wide variety of divers and grebes, gulls and shearwater, as well as the ubiquitous cormorant. Seabirds are attracted – of course – by fish, and a number of small fishing vessels operate along the coast near Portland Bill. If you are lucky, you might encounter one of these boats unloading its catch.

The rocky coastline is also the site of many **rock pools**, where children can have great fun trying to catch small crabs and other sea creatures. The rock itself was extensively quarried and many of the former quarry workings provide a safe environment for some **supervised rock climbing**.

The **lighthouse** is open to the public between April and September between the hours of 11 am and 5 pm, although it is closed on Fridays and Saturdays between April and June, and also on Saturdays between July and September. You can telephone 01305 820495 for further information.

3 Follow this path for ¾ mile down to the lighthouse at the tip of Portland Bill, passing through a collection of beach huts near journey's end. Bear right beyond the lighthouse to explore the southern tip of Portland Bill – including the Pulpit Rock – before returning to the car park.

Disused cranes along the way.

◆ Background Notes ◆

Thomas Hardy made frequent references to Portland in his novels. In *The Well Beloved*, he named it 'the Isle of Slingers', no doubt a reference to a skill possessed by the islanders in ancient times. Hardy also described Portland as 'the Gibraltar of Wessex'. **Portland Bill** has always been something of a ships' graveyard, so it comes as no surprise to discover George I issuing a patent for a lighthouse to be constructed hereabouts in 1716. The original pair of lighthouses contained enclosed lanterns and coal fires to warn passing ships of the dangers lurking around the Bill. Today's colourful 136 ft lighthouse was established in 1906. The light has an intensity of 674,000 candela, and a range of 25 sea miles. A red sector light warns mariners of the hazardous Shambles Bank lying three miles offshore. Visitors willing to negotiate the 153 steps can ascend the tower to secure what are perhaps the best views on Portland.

Portland has always been well known for its stone. From St Paul's Cathedral to the United Nation's Building in New York, uses have always been found for **Portland stone**. Although working dates back to the Middle Ages, it is only since the 17th century that extensive quarrying has occurred on Portland. The peak year for working was 1899, when 1,441 men were employed in over 50 quarries. Along the East Cliffs, this walk passes former workings, as well as disused cranes that once loaded stone into sea-barges for shipment to Weymouth harbour.

9

Lulworth Cove

Sea and Sand

On the beach at Lulworth.

The coastline along the Isle of Purbeck truly deserves its heritage status. This spectacular walk explores two of the area's best-known natural features. Lulworth Cove stands against a magnificent backdrop of vast chalk cliffs, whilst to the west lies Durdle Door. This vast natural arch has featured on many a postcard and calendar, and is responsible for keeping a number of pleasure boats fully employed during the summer months! This dramatic coastal excursion will surely prove a highlight of any visit to Dorset.

Kiddiwalks in Dorset

 Getting there *Take the A352 Wareham to Dorchester road and 2 miles west of Wareham turn onto the B3070, following it south for 8 miles to the car park at Lulworth Cove. NB: if the B3070 is closed due to MOD firing practice, the alternative route is via the A352 and Wool and the B3071.*

Length of walk 2 miles
Time 1½ hours
Terrain A steep ascent and descent on the coastal path between Durdle Door and

Lulworth Cove but nothing to deter young families from enjoying the experience.
Start/Parking The pay & display car park at Lulworth Cove (GR 821801).
Maps OS Outdoor Leisure 15 or OS Landranger 194.
Refreshments Lulworth Cove is a typical seaside resort with all manner of places to eat. I would recommend the Beach Café, which has a traditional seaside menu of open sandwiches and baguettes, cream teas and ice creams, along with the proprietor's famous Dorset home-made cakes.

The Walk

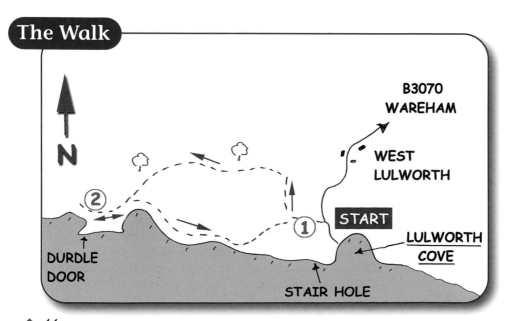

Lulworth Cove

1 Walk up to the top end of the car park, pass through a handgate and turn right to follow a fence on the right all the way around the foot of a hillside field. In 600 yards, pass through a handgate and follow the right edge of the field ahead uphill for 400 yards to another handgate and a tarmac lane leading to the Durdle Door car park. Turn left along this lane, and walk through to the car park. Beyond the end of this car park, follow the path downhill for ¼ mile to Durdle Door.

The view near Durdle Door.

◆ Fun Things to See and Do ◆

Either side of Durdle Door lie **fine sandy beaches**. It is well worth climbing down the steps to one or other of these beaches as a halfway break on this walk. If you intend doing this, however, don't forget to pack towels and beach gear to avoid the wrath of youngsters in your party! Failing this, simply walk back to Lulworth Cove and enjoy a pleasant few hours on the sand and shingle beach. There are pebbles and shells to collect, shallow waters to paddle in or – for the intrepid visitor – slightly deeper waters to swim in. It is even possible to take a **boat trip from Lulworth Cove** along the coast to Weymouth.

2 Having explored the beaches and rock formations, retrace your steps back towards the car park. In 200 yards, where the main path begins to climb uphill, fork right onto a side path waymarked to Lulworth Cove. Continue up to a handgate, before following the line of a fence on the right to a hilltop above Lulworth Cove. Having reached the top, take the path downhill to a handgate and the car park in Lulworth.

◆ Background Notes ◆

Lulworth Cove represents the classic oyster-shaped bay so beloved of geographers. The sea eroded a weak joint in the hard Portland limestone that lines the Dorset coast around Lulworth, enabling the waves to wear away the softer rocks that lay behind. The erosive power of the waves was only halted by a barrier of hard chalk, whose cliffs now form the backdrop to the Cove. Many yachts and small fishing vessels seek shelter in Lulworth Cove, continuing a long seafaring tradition. In the 18th and 19th centuries, smugglers brought their contraband ashore in this sheltered spot, with the barrels of liquor being hidden in nearby caves.

Alongside Lulworth Cove lies **Stair Hole**. This is a cove in the very process of formation. Once again, the sea has breached the hard Portland limestone and is slowly eroding the softer rocks further inland. Eventually, the destructive power of the waves will wear away the rocks separating Stair Hole from Lulworth Cove, forming one vast inlet from the sea.

Durdle Door is a vast rock arch, formed from near vertical beds of Portland stone that are joined to the mainland by Wealden clays. Arches evolve over time – waves initially wear away a joint in the rock to form a small cave. Wave action gradually attacks this small cave, eroding through the rock until the arch is formed.

Bockhampton

Nature Trail in Hardy Country

The heathland near Bockhampton.

A delightful walk into the heart of the countryside where the novelist Thomas Hardy grew up. Our steps lead us to the beautiful thatched cottage where Hardy himself was born in 1840. It is surrounded by a natural landscape that is home to deer, badgers, squirrels and all manner of other wildlife.

Kiddiwalks in Dorset

 Getting there *Initially, head for a roundabout on the north-eastern edge of Dorchester where the B3150 joins the A35. At this roundabout, take the unclassified road signposted to Stinsford and Bockhampton. In ¾ mile, at a crossroads, take the left turn to Hardy's Cottage. Follow this lane for ½ mile to a right turn to Hardy's Cottage, before taking the first right in just 100 yards into a visitors' car park.*

Length of walk 2½ miles
Time 2 hours
Terrain A relatively easy walk, with just one or two short hills

along the way so suitable for all children from 4 years and upwards.
Start/Parking The visitors' car park for Hardy's Cottage (GR 726922).
Maps OS Outdoor Leisure 15 or OS Landranger 194.
Refreshments There are no refreshment facilities on this walk. Why not drive into Dorchester, where there are any number of cafés and teashops, restaurants and bars? This will also give you the chance to visit the Dorset County Museum, which houses the largest Hardy collection in the world, including a reconstruction of his study.

The Walk

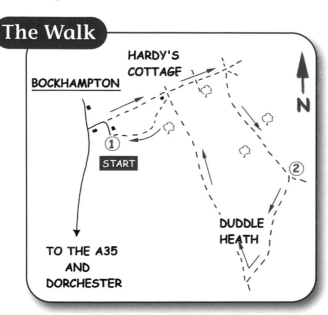

1 Follow the road out of the car park to a junction, turn right and walk along an unmetalled road for 350 yards to Hardy's Cottage. Continue ahead for a few yards to a crossroads just by Hardy's obelisk, and follow the path directly ahead, waymarked to Puddletown. In 200 yards, keep ahead at a crossroads. Ignoring a path coming in on the left – and another on the right – continue for 100 yards to a major junction of paths in a clearing. Take the first path going off on the right and, ignoring all left and right turns, follow the main path ahead for ¾ mile to a junction on open heathland.

2 Keep on the main path, which continues ahead – bearing right and dropping downhill – and walk on for 500 yards to a crossroads. Turn right, cross a stile and follow a waymarked footpath for ½ mile to a stile. Beyond this stile, take the path ahead,

◆ Fun Things to See and Do ◆

All around Hardy's Cottage lies mixed woodland and open heath, a landscape that is for ever associated with Dorset. In the car park, a series of **colourful information boards describe the shrubs and trees, the mammals and butterflies, the birds and fungi** that it might be possible to spot along the way. Roe and fallow deer inhabit this area, for example, whilst the kestrel and green woodpecker are just some of the birds that you might see flying overhead. A pair of field glasses should be obligatory on this particular walk. The children will enjoy looking out for animal tracks and droppings too. Badgers, for example, leave well-defined tracks and footprints that clearly show their long claws. The roe deer leaves what can only be described as slots in the ground, and you can even tell by the pattern of the markings whether the deer were walking or running! If you see a tree whose bark has been gnawed away, that is the sure sign of grey squirrels in the area, whilst empty acorn shells mean that the woodmouse has probably been this way.

Hardy's Cottage is owned by the National Trust, and is well worth visiting on this walk if you are here between April and October. Telephone 01297 561900 for details. Hardy's grandfather was involved in a small way with brandy smuggling, and added a narrow opening in the porch to keep his eye open for the excisemen!

waymarked to Hardy's Cottage, initially passing a pond on the left. In 350 yards, at a junction, follow the waymarked left turn back to the car park – or turn right if you wish to visit Hardy's Cottage, which is just 50 yards away.

Thomas Hardy's Cottage.

◆ Background Notes ◆

Thomas Hardy (1840–1928) was one of England's finest novelists and poets. His writing was inspired by the Wessex landscape in general, and the Dorset countryside in particular, which acts as an ever-present backdrop to his novels. An architect by training, his first literary success came in 1874 with the publication of *Far From the Madding Crowd*. Hardy's work has been described by one critic most succinctly: '... remarkable for the background contrast of richly humorous rustic characters, for the brooding intensity of human loves and hates played out before the harshly indifferent force of the natural world.'

In 1800, in the remote and wild setting of this Dorset heathland, John Hardy built a small 'cob and thatch' cottage that remained the family home for several generations. The Hardys were a firm of simple country builders, using old-fashioned materials and traditional methods, and the original three rooms of what is now **Hardy's Cottage** show far more quality in the building than the later extensions. But the cottage did not acquire its place among England's famous houses for the skilled craftsmanship employed in its construction, that honour coming 40 years later with the arrival of the builder's great-grandson, who was born in the middle bedroom, where he later worked at his desk on *Under the Greenwood Tree* as well as *Far From the Madding Crowd*. Hardy wrote of the property: 'It faces west, and round the back and sides high beeches, bending, hang a veil of boughs, and sweep against the roof.'

Milton Abbas

Picture Postcard

The main street through Milton Abbas.

Arthur Mee, in his *King's England* series, was clearly impressed by Milton Abbas. 'We come to it for its lovely street, but more than all for its old abbey, one of the jewels of Dorset. There can hardly have been a day since Alfred's grandson founded the abbey when it has not been beautiful.'

Beyond a delightful path that borders a fishing lake, the walk enters the grounds of Milton Abbey School whose premises are dominated by the well-known abbey itself. Founded by King Athelstan to commemorate the death at sea of his brother Edwin, the present huge 14th/15th-century church comprises only the chancel, tower and transepts, as the eastern chapels were demolished and the church nave was never built following a disastrous fire in 1309. Add a woodland path and hilltop views, and here is a delightful walk with interest at every turn.

Kiddiwalks in Dorset

11

Getting there *Initially, make for Winterborne Whitechurch, a village on the A354 Dorchester road, 5 miles south-west of Blandford Forum. In the village, head north on the unclassified road to Milton Abbas that leaves the A354 by the Milton Arms. In 2 miles, turn left into the centre of Milton Abbas – signposted to Milton Abbey – and park in the main street alongside the church.*

Length of walk 2½ miles
Time 2 hours
Terrain A gently undulating landscape, with one climb beyond Milton Abbey up through Pidgeon House Plantation. Suitable for children of four years and upwards.
Start/Parking The road outside Milton Abbas church (GR 807018).
Maps OS Explorer 117 or OS Landranger 194.
Refreshments There is a delightful thatched teashop in Milton Abbas's main street, as well as the quite excellent Hambro Arms pub.

❶ Continue walking down the main street in Milton Abbas and, at a junction in 300 yards, turn right along a side lane signposted to Milton Abbey. In 75 yards, turn left immediately before Lake Lodge and follow a footpath that soon borders a fishing lake, which lies beyond the fence on the left. In 400 yards, where the path enters the grounds of Milton Abbey School, keep ahead at a junction and follow a gravelled path all of the way around to the west door of Milton Abbey. Continue along the path past a former mansion – now part of the school – and turn right to emerge in front of the entrance to this grand building – now the school reception. Continue along an access road to the Abbey Tuck Shop, before continuing ahead past a series of classroom blocks and along a 'no entry' road (for cars) and out onto a lane.

❷ Turn left, and follow this lane for 150 yards to a path on the right, immediately before a private road leading to Delcombe Farm. Follow this path to the right for 350 yards up through

Charming almshouses passed on the walk.

The Walk

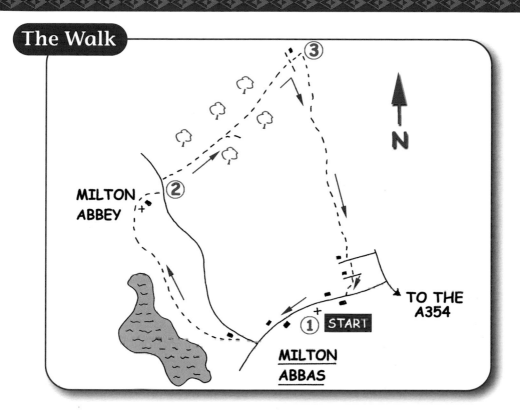

woodland to a wooden barrier, then walk on for 20 yards to a junction. Continue along the path ahead – ignoring the path going uphill on the right – and go on through the woodland for 300 yards to a junction of paths. Follow the unmetalled road ahead, passing through an old gateway, before turning right just past this gateway onto a bridleway.

3 Follow a short section of enclosed path, before continuing along the right edge of a large arable field. In 600 yards, in the far corner, pass through a gap in the hedge into the adjoining field. Walk across this – bearing left all the while – to a handgate opposite, before continuing down a path alongside a house to an estate road on the edge of Milton Abbas. Turn left for 20 yards to a telegraph pole – passing the Milton Surgery – then follow an enclosed path on the right down to another road. Turn right and, in 10 yards, left into a

11

◆ Background Notes ◆

The **attractive village of Milton Abbas** holds the distinction of being the first planned settlement in England. It was founded in 1780 when Lord Milton, Earl of Dorchester decided that the old village ruined the view from his new mansion at Milton Abbey. So he set about moving the entire village over a nearby hill. Sir William Chambers was the architect responsible for carrying out the Earl's wishes, and he created a delightful community of whitewashed and thatched cottages lining a broad street. Materials as diverse as broom, sedge, sallow, flax, grass, and straw can be used for thatching. Most common is wheat straw in the south of England, and reeds in East Anglia. Norfolk reed is especially prized by thatchers, although in northern England and Scotland heather was frequently used. Each cottage was fronted by a lawn, and a chestnut tree was planted between dwellings. The trees unfortunately did not withstand the ravages of time and disease, and had to be removed in 1953, but the cottages remain much as Chambers built them.

Milton Abbey was a Benedictine foundation, but only part of the church now survives and it is used as the Milton Abbey School chapel. The medieval church burned down in 1309, and rebuilding had barely begun at the time of the Dissolution of the Monasteries. In 1771, to make way for a new house, the 1st Baron Milton demolished the remaining abbey buildings, keeping only part of the church as a private chapel. The new house was designed by William Chambers and the gardens by Capability Brown. The abbey was originally founded by King Athelstan, and there are two medieval paintings of the king and his mother in the chancel.

Another of the church's benefactors was John Tregonwell, whose family came into the possession of the buildings following the Dissolution. Tregonwell fell from the roof of the church in a childhood accident, but his life was saved when his wide pantaloons filled with air and broke his fall. In thanks, he bequeathed his library to the church. The abbey is open at all normal daytime hours and although there is no admission charge, donations are welcome.

cul-de-sac. Follow this lane around to the right and, immediately before a property called Pine Ridge, turn left and walk steeply downhill on a path through woodland to reach the main street in Milton Abbas. Follow this road to the right, back to the church.

◆ Fun Things to See and Do ◆

The main street in Milton Abbas is lined with thatched properties so ask the children to count how many thatched cottages they can see.

In the middle of these thatched cottages is St James' church. To celebrate the millennium, **embroidered images of each pupil** at the local primary school were produced. These are on display in the children's corner in the church. There is also a rather **fine tapestry of the village of Milton Abbas**, with the various cottages, the church, the almshouses and many other landmarks shown. Having walked around the village, see how many of these landmarks the children can recognise.

Old churches are full of intriguing artefacts, and **Milton Abbey** is no exception. The marble monument to Lady Dorchester and her husband is interesting, as is a brass showing a kneeling man in Tudor dress. Look out too for the painting of King Athelstan – who founded the abbey – and his mother, as well as a very beautiful tabernacle shaped like a tower, made by a craftsman in wood over 500 years ago. Youngsters are always fascinated by the story of John Tregonwell (details in the church guide) who fell from the roof of the church and survived!

Sturminster Newton

Full Steam Ahead

The old market cross in the town.

Sturminster Newton on the River Stour, at one time a market town, lays claim to being the capital of the Blackmore Vale. Hardy called it Stourcastle in *Tess*, and there are indeed fragments of an ancient castle to justify the name. From the centre of Sturminster Newton, the trackbed of the former Somerset & Dorset Railway – now a cyclepath and footpath – is followed to the river, a mile to the east of the town. This is the location of Fiddleford Mill, with its impressive millstream and weir, as well as the local manor.

A delightful riverside path alongside the Stour is followed back into Sturminster Newton, with an opportunity to feed the ducks.

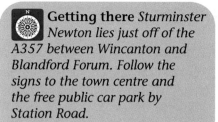 **Getting there** *Sturminster Newton lies just off of the A357 between Wincanton and Blandford Forum. Follow the signs to the town centre and the free public car park by Station Road.*

Length of walk 2 miles
Time Up to 2 hours
Terrain A flat and easy walk that follows a former railway trackbed

and fieldpaths alongside the River Stour.

Start/Parking Station Road car park in Sturminster Newton (GR 788142).

Maps OS Explorer 129 or OS Landranger 194.

Refreshments The meadow alongside the River Stour opposite Fiddleford Mill is quite the perfect spot for a picnic. Back in Sturminster Newton, there are pubs and cafés and restaurants aplenty.

The Walk

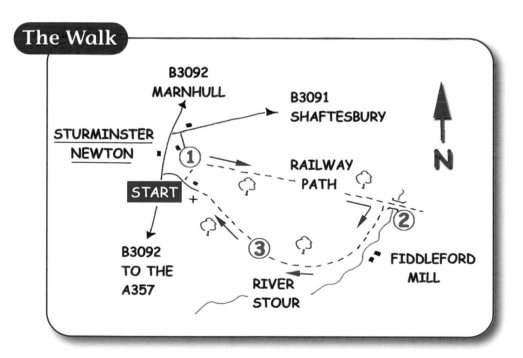

1 Walk down to the bottom corner of the car park and join the Railway Path, signposted to Fiddleford Manor and Mill. Follow this path for ¾ mile through to Fiddleford Bridge and the River Stour. Just before the bridge, veer right down to a handgate and the banks of the Stour.

◆ Background Notes ◆

As with so many rural towns, it was the market that gave Sturminster Newton its raison d'être, giving 'Stur' its nickname of 'the capital of the Blackmore Vale'. A market was held in the town as far back as 1272 and it was once **England's largest calf market**, but despite the best efforts of the Sturminster Market Action Group, the final one was held on Monday 30th June 1997, with the site being earmarked for housing and assorted commercial developments. No longer are Mondays distinguished by the 'farmer and his wife' coming from one of the many small dairies across the vale, the farmer to sell his cattle and the wife to buy the week's provisions.

It is not just the market that Sturminster Newton has lost in the past few decades. The town was connected to the national railway system in 1863 when the Dorset Central Railway completed the stretch of line from Blandford to Templecombe. It subsequently extended northwards to make an end-on connection with the Somerset Central Railway at Cole, thus becoming the much loved and still mourned **Somerset & Dorset Joint Railway**. There was even a special siding for the town's creamery, which at one time processed the milk from 122 local farms. Both this and the cattle market generated considerable traffic for the railway until the ubiquitous lorry took the business. This loss of goods traffic from the railway, and the increasing private car ownership, heavily influenced the closure of most of the line in 1966. The S&D lives on in the memory of older generations, 'swift and delightful' to its enthusiasts, whilst 'slow and dirty' to its critics. Perhaps the best-known train to come this way was the Pines Express, taking its weekly load of holidaymakers from the north of England to the south coast for their holidays each summer Saturday.

The former railway trackbed gives access to **Fiddleford Manor and Mill**. It was in the fields around the mill that a young William Barnes – the noted 19th-century Dorset poet – worked. Many of his poems – including one entitled *Leaves* – were probably inspired by his beloved River Stour. The mill house stands alone, reflected in the millpond that fills from the Stour as it cascades over a weir. It is a beautiful setting, with fishermen casting out beyond the river's yellow water lilies, and picnickers lazing within sound of the weir on summer days. The restored manor house is open to the public and is one of the oldest buildings in Dorset. In about 1355 the manor passed through marriage to William Latimer, sheriff of Somerset and Dorset in 1374 and 1380, and the late 14th-century Great Hall and Solar were built for him. Both rooms have 600-year-old timber roofs with collar-beam trusses and timber work of great complexity and beauty.

② Follow the river to the right – upstream – across two fields to the weir pool by Fiddleford Mill. A detour to the left across a footbridge will enable you to explore the mill and manor complex. For the main walk, cross a small footbridge in the end field boundary of the second field and enter a large riverside meadow. Bear half-right and walk across to a handgate in the far right corner of the field, before following the right edge of the next field for 75 yards past an old oak tree to another handgate.

③ Beyond this gate, walk across the middle of the next field to a handgate on the edge of Sturminster Newton. (Note – the right-of-way across these meadows runs some distance from the Stour. Many walkers,

The peaceful River Stour.

however, choose to follow a well-worn, unofficial path along the riverbank.) Beyond this handgate, follow an enclosed path waymarked to Penny Street. Follow this path through to a back lane in Sturminster Newton, turn right and, in 200 yards, follow a footpath on the right waymarked to the Station Road car park.

◆ Fun Things to See and Do ◆

The former railway trackbed brings the walk to the **River Stour and Fiddleford Mill**. Exploring the area around the mill – with its weir, sluices and footbridges – will certainly attract the interest of youngsters. Along the riverbank, keep your eyes peeled for flashes of blue – the kingfisher, one of our most beautiful of birds, is resident beside the Stour. The river is also home to all manner of wildfowl, including moorhens and coots, mallards and swans, so make sure that the children bring some old bread along to feed these ever-hungry creatures.

Poets are often inspired by the natural landscape. One of the most famous of Dorset's poets was William Barnes, who was born near Sturminster Newton in 1801. His poem *Vields by Watervalls* – 'Fields by Waterfalls' to us – could well be a description of the scene by the weir at Fiddleford Mill. Here are a few lines from this poem, written in dialect:

> Here below the bright-zunned sky
> The dew-bespangled flow'rs do dry,
> In woody-zided, stream-divided
> Vields by flowen watervalls.

Maybe the children – or indeed the adults – might feel stirred to **write a few lines of poetry** as you sit enjoying a picnic alongside the sparkling waters of the Stour.

13

Okeford Hill

Sitting on Top of the World

The Armada Beacon on Okeford Hill.

The Blackmore Vale, an area of gently undulating pastureland, stretches across the northern part of Dorset and was immortalised by Thomas Hardy as 'the land of little dairies'. The vale is set against a backdrop of the North Dorset Downs, open rolling hills with a patchwork of fields and small dark woodlands surrounding contrasting settled valleys. It is this downland high above Okeford Fitzpaine that is the focus of this walk, where the presence of a beacon should come as no surprise.

Along the way, our steps pass through ancient woodland as well as across the National Trust's Ringmoor property, where a series of humps and bumps on the ground are evidence of ancient settlement. A fine upland stroll with good views at every turn.

Kiddiwalks in Dorset

13

Getting there *Follow the A357 east from Sturminster Newton for 2 miles to New Cross Gate before heading south on an unclassified road to Okeford Fitzpaine. Having passed through the village, continue for 200 yards to a junction and turn left towards Winterborne Stickland. In 1 mile, at the top of a climb, turn right into the Okeford Hill car park and picnic area.*

Length of walk 2½ miles
Time Up to 2 hours
Terrain A relatively straightforward walk that follows well-defined tracks and paths around Okeford Hill. There is one short climb up through the woodland on the National Trust's Ringmoor property, an ascent that should pose few problems for active youngsters from age 4 and upwards.

Start/Parking The car park and picnic area on Okeford Hill (GR 812093).

Maps OS Explorer 117 or OS Landranger 194.

Refreshments The walk starts and finishes at a picnic site on Okeford Hill, which means that eating alfresco is an obvious choice! Should you be looking for a family-friendly pub, the Crown at Winterborne Stickland, 3 miles south of the picnic area, is a Grade II listed inn with a family room.

The Walk

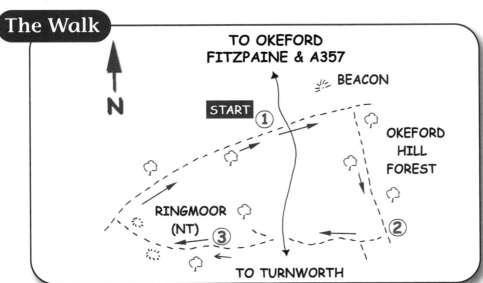

TO OKEFORD
FITZPAINE & A357

BEACON

N

START ①

OKEFORD
HILL
FOREST

RINGMOOR
(NT) ③

②

TO TURNWORTH

1 Leave the car park, turn right along the road and, in 20 yards, turn left along a bridleway signposted to Shillingstone. In 250 yards, just before an Okeford Hill Forest sign, turn right into a field – not right along the enclosed bridleway immediately past this field. Follow the left edges of two fields for ½ mile to the end of the second field, with an open view across a valley on the right.

2 In the corner of the second field, turn right and follow a track down the left edge of a field – ignoring an early left turn – to a handgate in the bottom corner of the field. Drop downhill in the next field – bearing right all the while – to a gate and road in the valley bottom. Cross the road and enter the National Trust's Ringmoor property. Just past the entrance gate, keep left at a fork and follow a well-defined path

◆ Fun Things to See and Do ◆

The woodland that forms part of the National Trust's Ringmoor property – as well as the Okeford Hill Forest – is awash with a **rich variety of flora** during springtime. Amongst the more common flowers are bluebells and primroses, wood anemones and celandines. The woodland also boasts a **wide range of tree species**, including oak and ash, beech and hazel. This is the perfect walk to enjoy, accompanied by a spotter's guide or two – ideally those that will enable youngsters to identify wild flowers and trees.

Ringmoor is also the site of an **ancient settlement**, dating back many thousands of years. All that remains to this day are a series of humps and bumps on the ground marking the location of a farmstead and field systems. It is interesting to try to work out some of the features of this long lost village by examining the raised circles and banks that lie on this open stretch of ground, maybe inspiring the budding archaeologists in your party.

uphill through woodland for 500 yards to a gate.

3 Beyond this gate, follow the main path ahead across the open ground of Ringmoor. In ½ mile, pass through a gateway and follow a track past a small pond and onto its junction with a major track – the Wessex Ridgeway. Turn right, and follow this track across the hilltop for ¾ mile before bearing left back into the Okeford Hill car park.

◆ Background Notes ◆

Okeford Hill is part of the Dorset Downs Area of Outstanding Natural Beauty. The Dorset Downs boast some of the finest chalk scenery in southern England, the downland forming an elevated 'backbone' of varied chalk landscapes. The county's website outlines the rich and diverse nature of this unique downland environment. Amongst the phrases that are used are 'dramatic scarps and steep-sided sheltered valleys' and 'species-rich grassland, complex coombes and valleys, spectacular views, prominent hillforts and other prehistoric features'.

High on this downland stands the **Armada Beacon**, enjoying a prominent location on a lofty hilltop perch above the Blackmore Vale. As the name suggests, this was but one of a series of beacons that would have illuminated the night sky some 400 years ago to warn of the approach of the Spanish Armada. In more recent times, these beacons have been lit to announce the Queen's Silver Jubilee in 1997 and the dawn of the new millennium. The beacon, whilst not lying on the actual walk route, can be accessed via a gate opposite the Okeford Hill picnic site.

The humps and bumps in the National Trust's **Ringmoor** property mark the site of an ancient Romano-British settlement. Pevsner describes 'a well-preserved prehistoric and Roman settlement, unusual in that it includes two small circular enclosures with internal occupation features' and goes on to record that there are '30 acres of associated Celtic fields'.

Hod Hill

Lofty Hilltop Perch

Exploring the Iron Age settlement on Hod Hill.

Hod Hill is the site of Dorset's largest Iron Age settlement, an area of some 54 acres that protected the important Stour Valley. The fort sits proudly atop a glorious chalk hill, with commanding views. To escape the heavy hand of history, this walk also includes a delightful woodland path along the banks of the River Stour. In springtime, this section of the route is awash with traditional English flora – primroses and bluebells, violets and celandines.

Kiddiwalks in Dorset

14

Length of walk 2½ miles
Time Up to 2 hours

Terrain An easy walk apart from one short – but very steep – climb onto Hod Hill itself. Be prepared for mud on the Stourside path in winter – wellies advisable. Suitable for children from age 4 and upwards.
Start/Parking Roadside by Holy Trinity church in Stourpaine (GR 860094).
Maps OS Explorers 117 and 118 or OS Landranger 194.
Refreshments The top of Hod Hill is quite simply an exceptional spot for a picnic. With chalk grassland and fine views, there are few better places to eat alfresco. Should you be looking for a fine hostelry, the White Horse Inn lies on the main A350 in Stourpaine, just a short drive from the start of the walk.

The Walk

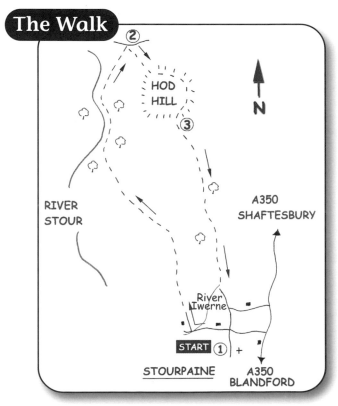

❶ Walk back along Manor Road, and take the first left turn into Havelins. Follow this road for 200 yards before bearing right into Hod Drive. Follow this lane – it soon becomes a track – for ½ mile until it drops down into Hod Wood. Continue through the woodland for ½ mile, the track bordering the River Stour.

2 Just before the path joins a lane, turn right to a handgate and the National Trust's Hod Hill property. Beyond this gate, turn right and follow the right edge of a steep hill up to a gate and the hillfort enclosure on the hilltop. Walk ahead along a track to the north-western corner of the hillfort and turn left onto the outer rampart. Follow the

The footpath alongside the River Iwerne.

ramparts around the north and east facing sides of the hillfort – about ½ mile.

3 At the south-eastern corner of the hillfort, pass through a handgate and follow a track for

◆ Fun Things to See and Do ◆

Water is always an attraction for youngsters, and there is a great deal of water along the way on this particular walk. The River Stour is far too deep and dangerous for a paddle, but do bring along some stale bread in your rucksack. There are usually a number of ducks along the river who are never averse to the odd snack! On the return to Stourpaine, our steps follow a footpath beside the River Iwerne. This tributary of the Stour is both clear and shallow, and will have children positively crying out for a paddle on warm days. As well as bits of stale bread, a towel is a must in the old rucksack too!

The ramparts and ditches of **Hod Hill fort** will provide an excellent battleground for youngsters to re-enact invasions from centuries past. The hilltop is also the perfect habitat for **unusual flowers** and a **wide variety of butterflies**. A spotter's guide book to butterflies, would be useful on this particular walk.

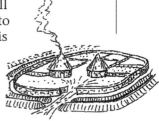

14

400 yards down to a footpath alongside the River Irwerne. Stay on this path for 250 yards until it joins Manor Lane in Stourpaine. This quiet lane takes you back to the church.

◆ Background Notes ◆

Stourpaine is a pretty place, with its collection of brick and flint cottages, as well as Holy Trinity church. Many of the houses carry the prefix 'Old' – the Old Schoolhouse and the Old Church House, for example – which speaks volumes about the decline of amenities in our rural villages.

There are many rivers called 'Stour' in England. It is likely that their name is very old, and is derived from the Celtic meaning 'strong or powerful one'. The longest **River Stour** flows through Wiltshire, Somerset and Dorset from springs and streams in all three counties, but with a definite starting point at Stourhead. A large part of its catchment is edged by chalk hills containing the Blackmore Vale where the river pushes its way through the clay, giving it a capacity to rise, rage and flood within a few hours – which certainly qualifies the river as strong and powerful.

The Stour Valley was a route of strategic importance in centuries past, with the summit of the majestic chalk **Hod Hill** providing an unequalled vantage point. The site was not impregnable, however, falling to the Second Augusta Legion during the first few years of the Roman conquest. The Romans constructed a fort of their own in the north-western corner of the site, where as many as 700 men and 250 horses were garrisoned. Whilst nothing remains of the Roman occupancy, the fort's ramparts and ditches present a truly impressive sight. The unimproved chalk downland on the hilltop means a rich array of flora – orchids and cowslips, for example – species that in turn attract a large number of butterflies including the marsh fritillary. An organisation called 'Butterfly Conservation' has identified as many as 36 types of butterfly on the hilltop, with all of the varieties listed and illustrated on their website: www.dorsetbutterflies.com

15

Fontmell Down

Upland Downland

The view from Fontmell Down.

Motorists travelling between Shaftesbury and Blandford Forum always face a dilemma. The main A350 road runs along the fringes of the Blackmore Vale – an undulating landscape – and it seems the obvious route to take when heading south. The road then deteriorates into a series of narrow bends as it skirts some majestic downland towering above the main thoroughfare – and many a traveller vows never to come this way again! The alternative is a steep winding climb through Melbury Abbas, before following a half-decent unclassified road across the hilltops further south into Dorset. The cause of these problems are Melbury Hill and Fontmell Down – vast areas of unimproved chalk downland where forever and a day it would be a crime to try to upgrade and improve the road system.

This quite majestic downland walk explores this corner of north Dorset where every superlative in the book will fail to convey the magnificence of the natural landscape. It is an excellent walk indeed.

Kiddiwalks in Dorset

15

Getting there *Head east from Shaftesbury on the A30 for just 150 yards before turning right onto the B3081. Follow this road south and continue onto an unclassified road south of Cann Common, the B3081 going off to the left – for 2 miles to Melbury Abbas. Take Spread Eagle Hill out of the village and, at the top of a steep climb, park on the right in the Fontmell Down car park.*

Length of walk 2 miles
Time 1½ hours
Terrain Although this walk explores high ground, it is a flat and easy route. If this sounds contradictory, it is because the car park is already at 775 ft above sea-level.
Start/Parking Fontmell Down car park (GR 886187).
Maps OS Explorer 118 or OS Landranger 183.
Refreshments The green open spaces of Fontmell Down are ideal for a picnic. There is an unusual alternative on the doorstep, however. Just a few minutes' drive from Fontmell Down is Compton Abbas Airfield, where visitors are very welcome to enjoy breakfasts or lunches or sandwiches – as well as desserts and cakes – whilst watching small planes taking off and landing.

The Walk

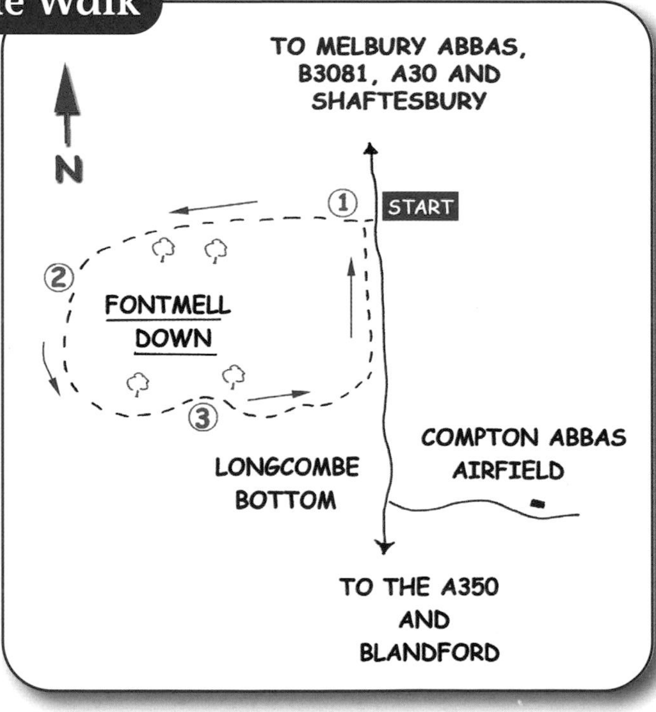

N

TO MELBURY ABBAS,
B3081, A30 AND
SHAFTESBURY

① START

②

FONTMELL
DOWN

③

LONGCOMBE
BOTTOM

COMPTON ABBAS
AIRFIELD

TO THE A350
AND
BLANDFORD

1 Pass through the handgate in the corner of the car park, and follow a fence on the left ahead across the hilltop. In ½ mile, having passed the woodland on the left, cross a stile in the fence on the left. Having crossed this stile, bear half-right and aim for some trees on the western skyline.

2 Beyond these trees, follow the line of the fence around the western end of Fontmell Down to a gate and stile on the left.

◆ Fun Things to See and Do ◆

 The skies above Fontmell Down are often filled with **birds of prey**, sparrowhawks, kestrels and buzzards. These are birds with superb vision that hunt for their food using their beaks and talons. The buzzard is easily identified by its size alone. The wingspan may vary between 48 ins to 60 ins with a body length of some 20 ins. Its plumage is a rich brown, with lighter markings beneath. It is a slow flier, and has little chance of catching its prey on the move. The usual tactics that it adopts are to perch motionless on a branch of a large tree, its markings being excellent camouflage. It is a patient bird, quite content to sit for hours at a time until a young rabbit, a rat or a mouse chances to pass beneath it. Then it will swoop down on to its unsuspecting prey.

Also flying in the sky above Fontmell Down are light aircraft from **Compton Abbas Airfield**. These small planes will fly low overhead, often performing a series of somersaults that resemble aerial gymnastics. It is worth visiting the airfield – where there is much to see and do – at the end of the walk. This is what the website (www.abbasair.com) has to say: 'Visitors will soon realise that this airfield does not cater purely for the aviator, but has something for everyone, including the young, and the not so young. It has a large car park with a grass area where the kids can play whilst mum and dad relax and watch the aerial activities against the backdrop of rolling hills.'

15

Scanning the sky for planes.

Cross this stile, and follow a fence on the left across the southern side of Fontmell Down for 600 yards to some woodland. Walk along the path to the right of the woodland to reach a stile, before continuing ahead across the open hilltop for 100 yards to some gorse bushes.

❸ Keep on the path as it bears slightly right to run around the head of Longcombe Bottom. Continue to a stile on the left on the far side of the field, just to the left of a clump of trees. Beyond this stile, follow a permissive path alongside the road back to the car park.

◆ Background Notes ◆

Set high on the chalk escarpment of the North Dorset Downs, **Fontmell Down** boasts stunning displays of chalk downland flowers and butterflies and spectacular views across the Blackmore Vale. In spring and early summer chalk milkwort, lady's bedstraw, bird's-foot trefoil, aromatic wild thyme and slad burnet provide a blanket of colour, as well as early gentian and clustered bellflower, early purple, bee and frog orchids. Later in the year hay rattle, restharrow, small scabious, pyramidal orchid, viper's bugloss and the delicate harebells burst into flower. Unusual butterflies found on this downland include the grizzled and dingy skippers, green hairstreak, dark green fritillary, adonis blue and brown argus. Adders and common lizards are also present. The scrub offers cover for the song thrush, blackbird, chaffinch, linnet, meadow pipit, willow warbler, yellow-hammer, skylark and green woodpecker while sparrowhawks, ravens, kestrels and buzzards are regularly seen above.

Also seen in the skies above Fontmell Down are low-flying aircraft, often performing a range of aerobatic feats. These light aircraft are based at **Compton Abbas Airfield**, nationally known as one of the most picturesque airfields in the UK. Situated at over 800 feet above sea-level, it commands spectacular panoramic views over some of England's most beautiful countryside. For those wishing to see the aviation side, many interesting vintage and historic aircraft are either based at or visit the airfield on regular occasions. Indeed, there is a small museum that features a number of restored and replica First and Second World War classic aircraft used in the motion picture industry, as well as movie props and general aircraft memorabilia.

Gore Heath

Disappearing Fast

The heathland near Wareham.

A heath is a very special habitat. Heaths only grow in a few areas around Britain – including Dorset – but these precious heathlands are fast disappearing. Similar heaths can be found in Europe but worldwide they are very rare ... in fact they are now rarer than tropical rain forests! Dorset's heathlands once covered over 50,000 hectares, stretching from the Avon Valley in the east to Dorchester in the west. Changes in agricultural practice, conifer planting, scrub encroachment, urban expansion and road building have all contributed to a reduction in area to about 7,000 hectares today.

This walk explores a small area of the heath north of Wareham, whose unusual wildlife means that a good spotter's guide and a pair of binoculars should be an absolute necessity on this walk.

Getting there *Follow the B3075 north from Wareham for 1 mile to the Lawson's Clump parking area in Wareham Forest.*

Length of walk 2½ miles
Time 2 hours

Terrain An easy walk that follows level paths and tracks.
Start/Parking Lawson's Clump parking area (GR 921909).
Maps OS Outdoor Leisure 15 or OS Landranger 195.
Refreshments There are a number of picnic tables alongside the parking area and, with no cafés or pubs on the route, a picnic is almost obligatory on this walk.

The Walk

N

WAREHAM FOREST

B3075 MORDEN

GORE HEATH

B3075 WAREHAM

① START

②

❶ Walk back towards the entrance to the car park, before turning left to follow a gravel track beyond a gate. Continue along this track – it soon bears left – and follow the main gravelled track in a northerly direction for 1 mile to a T-junction almost on the edge of the woodland. The main track winds its way through the woodland, and all side turns along the way should be ignored. Turn right, and follow a track for 600 yards to a distinct junction.

2 Follow the wider track to the right back into the heart of the woodland. Keep on this track for ½ mile until it emerges from the woodland to border an open field on the left-hand side. Continue along the track for another ½ mile to a point where a prominent track goes off on the right, with a gate on the left bearing a private property sign. Turn right here, and continue uphill to a junction of paths in

Pine cones can be spotted at every turn.

◆ Fun Things to See and Do ◆

A good deal of this walk passes through **coniferous plantations**, dominated by a large number of pine trees. The simple fir cone hides a fascinating tale. It is actually the female flower of the tree and contains the pine seeds; starting off as a flower, it hardens over anything between 12 and 24 months. The woody sections of the cone are called scales and are often pulled off by squirrels so that they can eat the seeds. You will no doubt find some of these stripped cones in Wareham Forest. Complete fir cones can be used as a way of forecasting the weather. On your return home, the children may be intrigued by putting a fir cone outside where they can observe it from time to time. When wet weather is coming, it will close up tightly in order to protect the seeds. A wide-open fir cone is a sure sign of sunny periods!

Heathland is particularly attractive to **birds** that like to nest on or near the ground including Dartford warblers, woodlarks and nightjars. Dorset heaths also boast all six species of **reptiles** found in the United Kingdom – adders, grass snakes, common lizards, slow worms, smooth snakes and sand lizards.

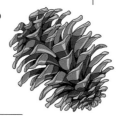

the middle of a mature clump of coniferous trees. Follow the path ahead, which drops downhill to a crosstrack.

Turn left, and retrace your steps along the track followed at the outset to return to the car park in 150 yards.

◆ Background Notes ◆

Having grown up on nutrient-poor, often sandy, acid soils, most **heathlands** have open, treeless areas, dominated by heather and gorse, a scrub or wooded component, stretches of bare ground and wet sections where the ground is boggy or there is open water. Sadly, well-managed heaths are rapidly disappearing, due not only to urban expansion and road building but also as a result of the development of coniferous plantations. This is all too evident on this walk where the name Gore Heath is almost something of a misnomer. Pockets of the ancient heathland remain, but the prevailing habitat is the woodland of Wareham Forest. Pine trees dominate this woodland, with the timber being grown for a range of commercial uses. Unfortunately, because coniferous trees can be planted in relatively dense stands, and because of their acidic decaying needles, it is difficult for other plant species to survive in such habitats.

Where the woodland has been cleared, the ancient heathland is able to re-establish itself. This is almost a throw back to the origins of this unique habitat. Most of Dorset's heathland was created by Bronze Age farmers, clearing woodland for agriculture. But the poor soils in some parts of the county made these areas unsuitable for crops and they were used largely for light grazing, providing the perfect conditions for some spectacular wildlife. In the past, heathland was undervalued and much has been lost to agricultural improvement, conversion to conifer forest and mineral extraction. In fact, only 15% of the heathlands that were present in 1750 in Dorset and the Poole Basin remain.

Badbury Rings

Running Around in Circles

An ancient oak tree near Badbury Rings.

Badbury Rings is an Iron Age hillfort protected by three concentric sets of ramparts and ditches. In a county renowned for its ancient relics, this must surely rank as one of the most impressive archaeological sites. Beyond this area – which Nikolaus Pevsner described as 'one of the great Wessex hillforts' – lies an area of woodland known as 'The Oaks'. The name is self-explanatory, whilst an information board provides background detail on what is the archetypal English tree, a species that lends its name to the official march of the Royal Navy. The whole is set against the rolling countryside of north-east Dorset, with many open views and far-ranging vistas along the way.

Getting there *Badbury Rings lie alongside the B3082, midway between Blandford Forum and Wimborne Minster. Follow the signs to the NT car park by this ancient monument.*

Length of walk 2 miles
Time 1½ hours
Terrain An easy walk on well-defined tracks and woodland

paths. There are no hills along the way.
Start/Parking The free car park at Badbury Rings (GR 960032).
Maps OS Explorer 118 or OS Landranger 195.
Refreshments There are no pubs or cafés on this walk, but the hillfort site provides an excellent picnic spot. The closest pub is the quite superb Anchor at nearby Shapwick.

The Walk

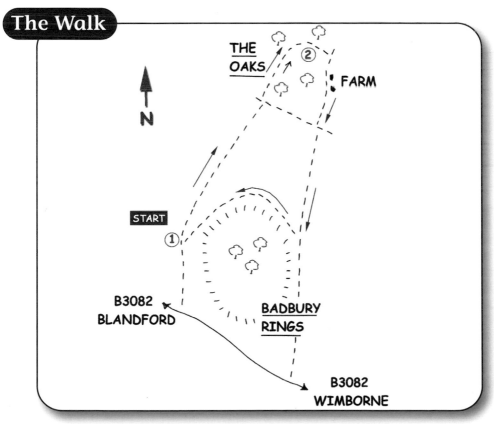

Kiddiwalks in Dorset

17

1 Walk up to the top left-hand corner of the car park, and follow a bridleway that borders Badbury Rings Point to Point track on the left. Walk along what is an enclosed chalky track for 350 yards, pass through a belt of trees and continue for 250 yards towards an area of woodland called The Oaks. At a junction

◆ Background Notes ◆

Badbury Rings represents one of the great Iron Age hillforts in Dorset. Situated on a chalk knoll, some 330 ft above sea-level, the site commands views that stretch from the Purbeck Hills to Cranborne Chase. Three rings of ramparts, the outer around 1 mile in circumference, protect the hilltop enclosure. Legend maintains that this was Mount Badon, where King Arthur defeated the Saxons. You might also like to ponder another piece of local folklore. The B3082, which runs along the southern fringes of the Badbury Rings site, passes through a quite magnificent beech avenue. There is supposed to be a beech tree for every day of the year – it is just a pity that the passing traffic makes it dangerous to put this theory to the test!

The Oaks – originally known as Sterley Bushes – used to provide grazing and shelter for young cattle, as well as supplying timber to the nearby Kingston Lacy Estate. Now the rotting wood from fallen trees provides the perfect environment for rare beetles and fungi. The National Trust manages this woodland to ensure the continued survival of this important habitat. Most oak trees in Britain are felled before they reach maturity. Unusually, the oaks here have been left to live out their natural lives and the fallen limbs are left to rot down. Oak polypore, a rare and endangered fungus, thrives in the rotting wood. This fungus provides an ideal breeding ground for a rare European beetle, *Sphaerites glabratus*, the first example of its kind found south of Yorkshire. A constant supply of dead and decaying oak is needed to maintain the feeding and breeding cycle of this insect, so much so that the National Trust often brings in dead wood from other areas.

100 yards into the wood, pass through a gateway opposite – to the left of an information board about oak trees – and follow a woodland path for 350 yards to a gateway at the exit from The Oaks.

2 Continue along a track to a junction, then turn right and follow a track for 350 yards to the next junction, just past King Down Farm. Follow the track opposite – waymarked to Badbury Rings – and continue for 400 yards to a belt of trees and two seats on a hilltop viewpoint. Just before these seats, turn right to a stile and the Badbury Rings site.

Head across to the inner rampart, turn right and follow the top of the rampart for 400 yards to a gravel path on the right. Follow this path back to the car park.

On the summit.

◆ Fun Things to See and Do ◆

Whilst the adults in the party might muse over the legend that King Arthur, disguised as a raven, lived in the woodland on the hilltop, youngsters can burn off excess energy on the ramparts **re-enacting King Arthur's escapades** against the invading Anglo-Saxons.

Rotting wood in The Oaks provides a rich breeding ground for all types of fungi, which in turn provides an ideal habitat for beetles and other insects, such as the rare oak polypore and the *Sphaerites glabratus* beetle that it attracts. Children will enjoy searching out all the different species. This is a very special habitat – so remind them to take nothing but memories and leave nothing but footprints.

Arne and Arne Heath

Wildlife Paradise

Deer grazing in Arne Nature Reserve.

Arne, 4 miles east of Wareham, is an isolated hamlet that lies in the heart of a vast area of heathland bordering Poole Harbour. This unique habitat, home to both the Dartford warbler and the smooth snake, has rightly been accorded nature reserve status. As well as taking in the rich flora and fauna, this walk extends to Shipstal Point, site of a Roman salt-making complex. A large part of the route follows an RSPB Nature Trail – permissive paths rather than rights-of-way – through level woodland and along coastal foreshore.

This is a truly memorable walk, through habitats that are home to 220 bird species, 31 mammal species, over 800 moth species and nearly 500 flowering plant species … in addition to 33 butterfly and 23 dragonfly species!

Arne and Arne Heath

Getting there *Follow the A351 from Wareham towards Swanage. At the first roundabout, 1 mile from Wareham, follow the left-turn signposted to Stoborough, Arne and the Toy Museum. Continue following the signs to Arne, which lies 3 miles along a cul-de-sac lane. In the village, park in the RSPB car park (fee payable for non-members).*

Length of walk 2 miles
Time Up to 2 hours
Terrain An easy walk that follows generally level paths in and around the Arne Nature Reserve.

The walk is suitable for youngsters of all ages, as well as all-terrain buggies.
Start/Parking The fee-paying Arne Nature Reserve car park (GR 973881).
Maps OS Outdoor Leisure 15 or OS Landranger 195.
Refreshments There is a picnic area in the RSPB car park in Arne. An equally attractive idea is to pack a picnic to enjoy on the beach overlooking Poole Harbour. The nearest pub is the King's Arms in Stoborough, on the road back to Wareham. This 400-year-old thatched hostelry welcomes families.

The Walk

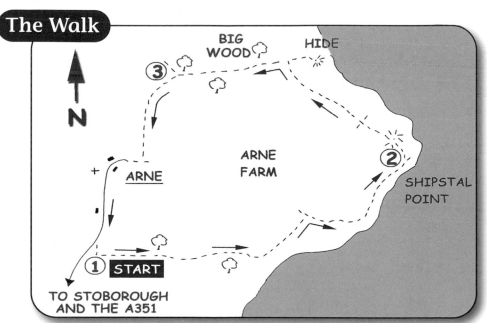

N

BIG WOOD

HIDE

③

ARNE FARM

ARNE

②

SHIPSTAL POINT

① START

TO STOBOROUGH AND THE A351

Kiddiwalks in Dorset

1 Walk to the top end of the car park and, beyond the ticket machine, continue along a track for 40 yards before turning right along a side path. Follow this path through an area of woodland for 600 yards, then continue along the right-of-way as it bears sharply to the left. Stay on the path as it heads in a northerly direction to a junction in some 250 yards, just past a section of board walk. At this junction, turn right and follow a path that bears left in 50 yards. Continue along this path as it borders a series of mudflats alongside Poole Harbour.

◆ Fun Things to See and Do ◆

 At Arne, you can discover a vast number of **different bird species**. The seasonal highlights include the Dartford warbler in song in spring, nightjars calling on the heath in the late evening in summer, little egrets reaching peak numbers for the year in autumn and dark-bellied Brent geese grazing in the fields in winter. A spotting guide – such as the *I-Spy Birds* book – would be fun on this walk. Along the way, keep a lookout for the deer that make the woodland their home. They are so used to human visitors that, if you keep still, they will come within touching distance!

Shipstal Point has a **fine sandy beach** overlooking Poole Harbour. This is a perfect spot to rest and linger awhile along the way, a place for a picnic and a paddle – so be sure to pack a towel for this walk.

At journey's end, the Arne **World of Toys** collection, Dorset's only toy museum, is certainly worth a visit and appeals to adults as well as children. The elaborate array of exhibits includes boats and steam engines, toy soldiers and teddy bears. The museum is open from April to September in the afternoons, but is closed on some Mondays and Saturdays. Telephone 01929 552018 for further details.

The beach overlooking Poole Harbour.

2 In 250 yards, where a path veers right down to the beach at Shipstal Point, follow the stepped path ahead that climbs uphill to a fine viewpoint across Poole Harbour. Continue along the path – it soon bears left away from Poole Harbour – to reach a viewpoint on Shipstal Hill. Drop down the far side of the hilltop viewpoint to a crossroads of tracks, before keeping directly ahead for 300 yards to a T-junction. Detour to the right to visit a hide overlooking Poole Harbour. For the main walk, keep left and follow the main path ahead – ignoring one left turn and one right turn – for 250 yards until, at the foot of a slope, it reaches a junction.

3 Keep left here, and follow the path up out of woodland to a point where it bears left and becomes a grassy ride. Stay on this ride for 200 yards to a handgate, and take a track to the right up towards a property in Arne. Keep on the track as it bears left and becomes a metalled lane in front of Arne church. Follow this lane along to a junction by the World of Toys museum, and then take the path that forks left back down to the car park.

◆ Background Notes ◆

The **Royal Society for the Protection of Birds** is a UK charity working to secure a healthy environment for birds and other wildlife, helping to create a better world for us all. With over one million members, it is the largest wildlife conservation organisation in Europe and its work focuses on the species and habitats that are in the greatest danger.

As you walk around the **RSPB's Arne Nature Reserve** you will see a variety of habitats including marshy woodland, saltmarsh, a sand spit and crumbling cliffs. From the high point on the trail – Shipstal Hill – the many landmarks in the locality can be identified from a very useful topograph. The view across Poole Harbour is certainly a breathtaking outlook! On the fringes of Big Wood, overlooking Poole Harbour, lies a strategically placed RSPB hide. The sharp-eyed visitor may well be rewarded with sightings of the cormorant, grey heron, curlew, oystercatcher, shelduck and redshank. A pair of field-glasses is an almost obligatory accessory on this walk.

Back in the village of Arne, it is worth spending a few minutes exploring **St Nicholas' church**. Although dating back to the 13th century, the building has been the subject of much alteration during the 19th century. Perhaps the highlight is the view from the altar window, encompassing a large part of Poole Harbour.

Worth Matravers

Rock and Roll

Looking towards Winspit.

The prosperity of the Isle of Purbeck was – before the advent of the cash crop known as tourism – based upon the local stone quarries. Purbeck limestone is still used to this day for flooring material and paving stones, as well as in the construction of drystone walls. Worth Matravers was a centre of this industry, with a number of quarries dotted around the edge of what is one of the prettiest villages on the Isle of Purbeck.

From Worth Matravers, this walk drops down through a delightful valley to Winspit, where the rolling waves of the English Channel come crashing in on the local rocky cliffs. Winspit itself is the site of some of the more dramatic stone workings in the area, with quarries and caverns burrowing away into the cliff faces. The coast path is followed along the clifftops to Seacombe – the location of yet more quarrying activity in centuries past – before another delightful dry valley returns the walker to the welcome delights of the Square and Compass in Worth Matravers.

Kiddiwalks in Dorset

 Getting there *Leave the A351 Wareham to Swanage road just east of Corfe Castle, and follow the signposted road to Worth Matravers. In 3 miles, just as you enter the village, there is a public car park on the right-hand side.*

Length of walk 2½ miles
Time 2 hours

Terrain A relatively challenging walk, with a steep ascent on the Coast Path, as well as a climb back into Worth Matravers. Keep youngsters firmly under control on the coastal section of the walk. Best suited for those aged five and over.

Start/Parking The visitors' car park in Worth Matravers (GR 974777).

Maps OS Outdoor Leisure 15 or OS Landranger 195.

Refreshments The Square and Compass in Worth Matravers is an excellent pub serving home-made pasties and real ales. It also has a front garden that is home to all manner of artefacts connected with the quarrying of Purbeck limestone.

The Walk

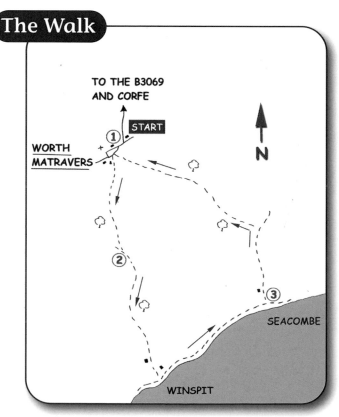

1 Leave the car park, turn right and walk down to a junction by the Square and Compass. Turn right and, in 100 yards, at a junction by a green and duckpond, fork left off of the main road. Follow a lane along the left-hand side of the green, before taking the second left turn by a property called 1 London Row. Walk down past a rank of cottages and, just by the last property, fork left along a gravelled footpath to a handgate. Beyond this gate, walk along a well-worn path down through a valley bottom field to a handgate on the right at the far end of the field. On the other side of the gate, follow a path down to its junction with a wide track.

2 Stay on this track for ½ mile down towards the coast at

◆ Background Notes ◆

The original prosperity of **Worth Matravers** was built upon the local quarries, where Purbeck Stone was cut and hewn. The industry even influenced the name of the village inn – the Square and Compass – a reference to the quarrymen's tools. The local buildings are all fashioned from Purbeck Stone, a grey, somewhat austere material. St Nicholas' church is worth exploring if for no other reason than to discover the grave of one **Benjamin Jesty**. This local man was a pioneer of cow vaccination, some 20 years before Edward Jenner, and is remembered on his memorial stone thus: '... and who from his great strength of mind made the Experiment from the Cow on his Wife and two Sons.' Their reaction is not recorded!

Winspit is the site of a disused cliff quarry. Layers of stone were extracted, with vast Purbeck Stone pillars being left to support the roof. In places, the strata can be seen buckling under the weight. These old workings are dangerous places and it is definitely better to look at them from afar! The stone was loaded directly into sea-barges for transhipment to Swanage, from where it was taken on to London. The quarries and caverns were also home to another local industry – smuggling. One notable local smuggler was **Isaac Gulliver** from Worth Matravers itself. His generosity in sharing his spoil amongst the villagers made him a highly respected figure in the community. The quarrymen and the smugglers have long gone, leaving today's disused quarry as a nesting place for a large colony of bats.

Winspit. On reaching a warning sign about the cliffs and quarries, turn left along the Coast Path towards Seacombe – having first made the obligatory detour down to the coast at Winspit. Follow the Coast Path steeply uphill to a handgate and hilltop field. Beyond this gate, turn right and walk beside a fence on the right across a field bordering the coast for 500 yards. In the far corner of the field, pass through another handgate and stay on the clifftop path for 100 yards to a stile. Beyond this, turn right and follow a fence on the right across a field to another stile. Over this stile, continue on an enclosed path to reach a handgate on the right. Pass through this gate and drop

Tremendous views greet the walker.

down some steps into the valley bottom.

3 A detour to the right will bring you to the coast at Seacombe. For the main circuit, turn left and follow a path through the valley, walking away from the sea. In 350 yards, at a marker post, fork left off the main path to follow the path waymarked to Worth. Cross a small footbridge over a stream, and continue along the length of a field to a handgate in the end field boundary. Climb the hillside ahead to a stile and, in the next field, follow the right-hand field boundary to a stile in the corner of the field. Cross the field ahead – dropping down initially into a valley – to a stile in the opposite field boundary in front of some properties. Beyond this stile, follow an enclosed path along to a lane. Turn right up to the duckpond, then turn right again to reach the Square and Compass before going left to return to the car park.

◆ Fun Things to See and Do ◆

Around the Winspit quarry site, there are a number of rocks and boulders that are great fun for some **safe rock scrambling.** If you are lucky, you might be doing this walk at the same time as climbers are scaling the local cliffs. This is one of the more exciting sporting activities to enjoy watching!

As you walk around Worth Matravers and the surrounding countryside, the children could see how many uses for **Purbeck Stone** they can spot. If they are interested in exactly what went on at these quarries in years gone by, then the Square and Compass at Worth Matravers has all manner of artefacts relating to the industry.

Winspit is a wonderful place for spotting **seabirds.** Amongst the species that local bird-watchers have recorded are the ring ouzel and Sabine's gull, as well as the firecrest and hawfinch. Be sure to bring along a good spotter's guide as well as a pair of binoculars.

Pentridge and Bokerley Ditch

On the Border

Martin Down National Nature Reserve.

Pentridge lies right up in the north-eastern corner of Dorset, a stone's throw from the Hampshire border. It is a pretty place, lying at the end of a quiet cul-de-sac lane in the shadow of Pentridge Hill and Penbury Knoll. To the east of the village, sitting astride the county boundary, is a vast earthwork known as Bokerley Ditch, an impressive Romano–British boundary. This ancient monument in turn borders Martin Down – just over the border in Hampshire – a vast area of unimproved chalk downland and grassland. Its status as a National Nature Reserve provides a clue as to the rich flora and fauna associated with this unique habitat. All of these elements combine to form a delightful walk that is quite literally 'on the border'.

Pentridge and Bokerley Ditch

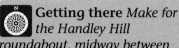 **Getting there** *Make for the Handley Hill roundabout, midway between Blandford Forum and Salisbury, where the A354 forms a junction with the B3081. Continue towards Salisbury for 1¼ miles, before turning right along a cul-de-sac lane to Pentridge. In ¾ mile, at a T-junction in the village, turn right. In 250 yards, turn right up a side lane – it shortly becomes unmetalled – and drive past the church on the left to a rough parking area in front of a cottage and the church hall.*

Length of walk 2¾ miles

Time 2 hours
Terrain An undulating landscape, with one or two gentle climbs along the way.
Start/Parking The parking area adjacent to Pentridge church (GR 033178).
Maps OS Explorer 118 or OS Landranger 184.
Refreshments There are no cafés or pubs in Pentridge, so a picnic to be enjoyed on Martin Down is highly recommended. The closest pub is the Roebuck in the village of Sixpenny Handley. Drive back to the A354, turn left and continue for 1¼ miles to the Handley Hill roundabout before turning right along the B3081 into Sixpenny Handley.

The Walk

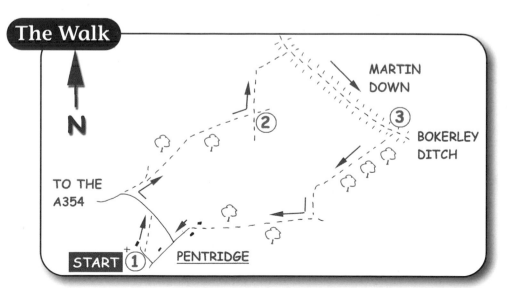

❶ Pass through a gate by the parking area into an arable field, turn left and follow the left edge of this field up past the village hall to a gate in its top corner. Join a lane, turn left and follow the lane for 200 yards to a left-hand bend. On this bend –

shown on the OS map as Peaked Post – turn right along a bridleway. Keep right at a fork in 150 yards, and continue for 600 yards to a junction of paths.

❷ Walk ahead, and opposite the enclosed path continues in an

◆ Fun Things to See and Do ◆

Bokerley Ditch, just to the east of Pentridge, represents a miniature version of Hadrian's Wall and youngsters can burn off excess energy recreating Anglo-Saxon forays into enemy territory.

Alongside the ditch is Martin Down, a vast area of chalk grassland that is home to any number of **butterflies and birds**, as well as a variety of rare plants and flowers. Notable plants found in the area include bastard toadflax, field fleawort, early gentian and lesser centaury. Twelve orchid species have also been identified, including burnt-tip, green-winged, greater butterfly and frog. Be sure to bring a spotter's guidebook on this walk.

Churchyards often contain **fascinating old tombstones**, and St Rumbold's church at Pentridge is no exception. You might spot the grave of Paul Robert Owen, the scientist, or William Walters Sargant, the writer and physician. There is also the tomb of Charles Richard Jacobs of the 5th Wiltshire Regiment who died on active service in 1915. And see if the children can discover a grave that is older than the 1745 one I spotted – that will prove a real challenge! Inside the church, have a look at the kneelers. These are hand-crafted with delightful rural designs – pheasants, cockerels, tractors, lambs, horses and even a trusty Landrover!

Rolling downland is a feature of this route.

easterly direction. Do not follow this path – just to its left is a gateway bearing a bridleway sign. Pass through this gateway, and follow the left edge of the field ahead for 300 yards to a point where a track comes in on the left. At this point, turn right and walk across the arable field to reach Bokerley Ditch on its far side and Martin Down National Nature Reserve. Drop down through the ditch to a grassy path and turn right. Follow the grassy path for ½ mile, all the while bordering Bokerley Ditch, until an area of woodland appears over on the right-hand side.

3 At this point – by a Martin Down Reserve sign – turn right, pass through the ditch and follow an enclosed path that borders the woodland on the left and an arable field on the right. In 500 yards, where the woodland ends, pass through a gateway and walk across the right-hand edge of a hillside field. In the corner of the field, turn right and walk down a grassy ride to a handgate by some farm buildings. Walk ahead to another handgate, then follow a grassy track to the next gate before following a farm road downhill to its junction with a lane by Whitey Top Farm. Turn left and follow the lane ahead to a junction in Pentridge. Walk ahead for 250 yards, before turning right along the lane leading to the church and the parking area.

◆ Background Notes ◆

Pentridge enjoys a secluded location. Its Celtic place-name literally translates as 'hill of the boars', testimony to the ancient origins of this settlement. The village featured as 'Trantridge' in Thomas Hardy's *Tess of the d'Urbervilles*. The literary connections continue in the village church, named after the 8th-century Celtic Saint Rumbold. A tablet on the south wall of the nave commemorates Robert Browning, the first known forefather of Robert Browning the poet. Their son Thomas, born in 1721, was the poet's great-grandfather. The poet, incidentally, always spoke of Pentridge as 'the cradle' of his family.

Pentridge sits on the fringes of Cranborne Chase, an area that is literally riddled with archaeological remains. One of the more spectacular relics on the Chase is **Bokerley Ditch**, an earth rampart of Romano-British origin. This 6-mile-long line of defence, running between Blagdon Hill and the high ground that forms the northern part of the Chase, was constructed to protect the tribesmen of Dorset from Anglo-Saxon invasions. At one point, the ditch physically blocked the Roman road running from Dorchester to Old Sarum.

Bordering Bokerley Ditch is **Martin Down**. This National Nature Reserve contains a number of fine downland habitats, which include herb-rich turf, longer grassland, scrub, developing woodland and heath. Martin Down is renowned for its unusual species of butterfly, among them silver-painted skipper and Adonis blue. Ornithologists should also keep their eyes skinned for such feathered varieties as the nightingale, the hen harrier and the lesser whitethroat.